YORK NOTES

General Editors: Professor A.N. Jeffares (*University of Stirling*) & Professor Suheil Bushrui (*American University of Beirut*)

Jbs
Tabridge
1991

Elizabeth Gaskell

NORTH AND SOUTH

Notes by Anahid Melikian

BA (WAGNER COLLEGE) PHD (WISCONSIN)
Assistant Professor of English,
American University of Beirut

LONGMAN
YORK PRESS

D0255847

YORK PRESS
Immeuble Esseily, Place Riad Solh, Beirut.

LONGMAN GROUP UK LIMITED
Longman House, Burnt Mill, Harlow,
Essex CM20 2JE, England
Associated companies, branches and representatives
throughout the world

First published 1980
Third impression 1991

ISBN 0-582-78183-3

Produced by Longman Group (FE) Ltd.
Printed in Hong Kong

ᏝNᏝ

ᴧꞩ6244Ꭺ

Contents

Part 1

Introduction

The life of Elizabeth Gaskell

Elizabeth Cleghorn Stevenson was born in London on 29 September 1810. She was the eighth and last child of William Stevenson and his wife Elizabeth. William Stevenson was a Scot. He was a Unitarian minister at Failsworth near Manchester (see page 8). He resigned his orders and position on conscientious grounds; that is, he did not agree any more with the teachings of his Church, and his conscience did not permit him to continue in his work. He had to find another income to support his family. First he tried scientific farming, then he turned to literary work, and finally acquired the post of Keeper of the Treasury Records. This was a government post which brought him to London, and this is where Elizabeth was born. Elizabeth's mother was also a Unitarian. She came from Cheshire, a county in the north west of England, and was related through her family, the Hollands, to some prominent English families, such as the Wedgwoods and the Darwins. She died when Elizabeth was only thirteen months old, and Elizabeth was brought up by a maternal aunt who lived in Knutsford, a small town in Cheshire. This is where she grew up. She came to know this place, its people and its customs very well. Later she was to use some of her Knutsford experiences, and some of its places and characters, in her novel *Cranford,* which for a long time was her most popular book.

From 1825 to 1827 she studied at Mrs Byerley's school at Avonbank, in Stratford-upon-Avon. She then went to live in London, where she nursed her father until his death in 1829. During this London period she stayed for a while with an uncle and probably had a chance to see something of the fashionable life of London which she later described in *North and South.* After London, she went to stay with other relatives, the Turners, at Newcastle upon Tyne, and during the cholera epidemic in 1831 she went to Edinburgh with Anne Turner. Later she visited and stayed with Anne's sister in Manchester; this lady's husband was the senior minister of Cross Street Unitarian Chapel. He had a young colleague named William Gaskell. It was not long before William proposed to the beautiful and vivacious young woman, and in August 1832 he and Elizabeth were married. That Elizabeth was beautiful, all her portraits testify. And we know from her letters and the comments of her contemporaries that she was lively and attractive, sociable and intelligent, interested in everything, and with a ready sympathy for others. It is not surprising, therefore, that William Gaskell was attracted to her so quickly.

William Gaskell was born in 1805. He was educated at a dissenting academy (that is, an institution of higher learning founded by a dissenting group), at the University of Glasgow, and at the Unitarian Manchester College in York. In 1828 he came to Manchester as assistant to the senior ministers at Cross Street Unitarian Chapel. He stayed in Manchester till the end of his life, eventually becoming senior minister himself.

Manchester at that time was not only a growing industrial city, but a city which was culturally and intellectually very much alive. Concerts, lectures, art exhibitions, often supported by the money of the industrialists, contributed to the life of the city. The Gaskells shared in this life, and had many friends among the prominent citizens.

They lived in Manchester for the rest of their lives. They had several children of whom four daughters survived; the only son died when he was a baby. This loss left Mrs Gaskell in a very depressed state. It is said that at this stage her husband encouraged her to write, to help her to get over her depression. She followed his advice, and the result was the novel *Mary Barton.* This was in 1848. *Mary Barton* was widely read, and Elizabeth Gaskell became an established writer. She had already written a number of short stories, but this was her first novel. In the years that followed, she kept on writing, both novels and short stories. Many of her novels appeared in serial form first. For example, *Cranford,* her most popular novel, first appeared in *Household Words,* running from September 1851 to May 1853. *Wives and Daughters,* her last novel, was originally published in *The Cornhill Magazine,* running from August 1864 to January 1866. Both novels appeared in book-form as soon as they were completed. Others were published in book-form from the start, for example *Ruth* (1853) and *Sylvia's Lovers* (1863). She wrote one biography, *The Life of Charlotte Brontë,* which was published in 1857.

Besides writing and travelling, Mrs Gaskell led a busy life as the wife of a minister and the mother of four daughters. Their house was always full of visitors, famous people such as Florence Nightingale,

Charles Dickens and his wife, and Charlotte Brontë; and others, who were not famous, but who were good friends. Apart from being a busy hostess, she was involved in many activities which are the duty of a clergyman's wife: Sunday schools, bazaars, social welfare, and other similar occupations.

Her husband was busy as well. Besides his duties as a minister, he was a lecturer and professor of English History and Literature and Logic in various institutes and colleges. He was a writer and editor, and very active in social work. He was prominent in most Unitarian societies. They seem to have had a happy and active life together. Although he was a man who often liked to be alone, and she was a sociable and warm woman, he allowed her more freedom and independence than the average Victorian husband did. For example, under the law he had the right to control her earnings. But it is clear that he did not insist on this right, for Mrs Gaskell travelled freely and widely, and, obviously, must have spent a lot of money that way. With the earnings of her last book, *Wives and Daughters*, she bought a house for her husband to retire to. A few weeks after they moved into it she died very suddenly, on 12 November 1865.

Social background

Mrs Gaskell lived at a time of great political and social change in England. This change was coming about as a result of the Industrial Revolution. Many people moved from the country to cities to find work in the new factories, and this caused the growth of the great industrial cities, such as Manchester, in which Mrs Gaskell lived most of her adult life ('Milton' of *North and South*). Another result of the Industrial Revolution was the rise of the new rich and powerful merchant and manufacturing class. This brought with it, of course, a corresponding class of workers, and many problems arising from the conflict between these two groups. There were also changes and reforms in political life, as more and more people (men, not women) demanded, and were granted, the right to vote, which made a change in the power structure inevitable. This, in turn, brought about a challenge to the class system, and an increasing social mobility, which meant that a hard-working man who made a lot of money in business could raise himself socially.

Mrs Gaskell knew all this at first hand. She had grown up in the country, in the small village of Knutsford, and knew that conservative

society intimately. She described it amusingly and with great observation in *Cranford*. When she married and moved to Manchester, she
acquired first-hand experience of the life of the workers,- and the
problems arising out of unsatisfactory labour-employer relations,
because as the wife of a clergyman she often visited the homes of the
poor. In her first novel, *Mary Barton,* she described the sufferings of
the working class at the hands of unscrupulous factory owners. In
North and South she made up for this by presenting a humanitarian
manufacturer, who is willing to learn from his workers, and is
successful in establishing good relations with them. We must remember that this is before all the labour laws were passed. By the end of
the nineteenth century many labour laws had been passed which
improved the condition of the workers, and weakened the power of the
employers.

Mrs Gaskell was not the only writer of her day to be concerned with
problems of this kind. The novels of Charles Dickens (1812-70), which
deal with these problems, are well known. Among the most famous
are *Hard Times* (1854), and the more popular *Oliver Twist* (1837-8).
Other less-known novelists, such as Charles Kingsley (1819-75), also
tackled these problems. Thomas Carlyle (1795-1881), the social critic
and historian, wrote several books which influenced novelists and
politicians, among them Mrs Gaskell.

Religious background

Because Elizabeth Gaskell was the wife of a Unitarian clergyman, and
also the daughter of a former clergyman, and because *North and
South* starts with the religious conflict in the mind of the heroine's
father, it is necessary to say a few things about the religious situation
of her day.

The 'Established Church' of the country was the Church of England.
But the groups outside it, known as non-Conformists (because they
did not conform to the Thirty-nine Articles of the Church of England)
were becoming steadily stronger. The Unitarian Church was such a
church. It had been started in England in the eighteenth century. It
was a church with liberal doctrines, which rejected the Christian
doctrine of the Holy Trinity, but did base its teachings on the Bible.
In Mrs Gaskell's novels, for example, the religious emphasis is on the
New Testament teaching of love and forgiveness, and the importance
of the individual. The members of the Unitarian Church came mainly

from the intellectual and the wealthier classes. Because, like other non-Conformists, they were excluded at first from the schools and established universities, Oxford and Cambridge, they had been forced to found their own. This is why William Gaskell had attended a 'dissenting academy' (another word for 'non-Conformist') and a Scottish university.

A more influential movement with a larger number of followers was the Evangelical movement within the Church of England. The Evangelicals had been influenced by John Wesley and his Methodist Movement, and had brought new life into the church. They were active in all areas of life where reform was necessary. They were active on behalf of the poor and under-privileged, and they used their influence to abolish slavery, to establish schools, and to spread literacy among adults. It was also largely thanks to them that the working classes had learnt to organise themselves.

The Methodist Movement had been forced to leave the Church of England. But they continued outside the Church, as a non-Conformist church, to influence for the good the religious, social and educational life of all classes.

Literary background

Mrs Gaskell was the contemporary of Dickens, Thackeray, George Eliot, the Brontë sisters. She felt at home with her time and her readers, and found enough material in the world around her to shape into novels. But she and her contemporaries were not uncritical of their age. As we shall see in *North and South,* Mrs Gaskell was aware of the evils of the Industrial Revolution, the weakness of the Government at that time in enforcing industrial laws, the hostility that existed between the labourers and their masters, and the misery of the poor. As the author of 'social novels' or 'novels with a purpose', Mrs Gaskell can be compared to the best of her time. She knew how to portray the misery and the problems of a group or a class by presenting the lives of individuals. She made those individuals real and interesting enough to enable them to exist apart from the problems which they represent.

The nineteenth century was a great age for the novel in England. Mrs Gaskell, therefore, was lucky in having the example of other, often better, novelists, to follow, and also in finding a ready-made readership for her novels. Her sympathy, her intuition, her fluent style and interesting plots made her popular in her day, and modern readers will also enjoy her and find her interesting. It is a pity, however, that these good qualities should have hidden the fact that she was also a novelist whose novels were carefully constructed, and who developed a narrative technique which made her later novels stand with the best of her time.

A note on the text

North and South was originally published in serial form, in the weekly *Household Words,* which was edited by Charles Dickens. It ran into twenty-two weekly instalments, from September 1854 to January 1855. In June 1855 it was published in book form, in two volumes, by Chapman and Hall. This first edition differed slightly from the serialised version in being somewhat longer. Mrs Gaskell added the two chapters (45 and 46) which deal with Margaret's visit to Helstone with Mr Bell; and she lengthened the original last chapter into four. The author's original intention was to call the novel *Margaret Hale,* but Dickens persuaded her to change this to the present title.

Six editions of the novel appeared in Mrs Gaskell's lifetime. She probably revised the second edition somewhat. This is the one that was used by the German publishing house of Tauchnitz when they included it in their British Authors series in that same year, 1855. During her lifetime there were also two American editions, and before the end of the century the novel was reprinted over ten times. *North and South* appears of course in the collected editions of Mrs Gaskell's works *(The Novels and Tales,* 1872-3; *The Works,* Knutsford edition, 1906; and *The Novels and Tales,* 1906-9). It appeared in Everyman's Library in 1914, and in several other English and American editions in this century.

The present critical essay is based on the Penguin edition (1970), edited by Dorothy Collin, with an introduction by Martin Dodsworth.

Part 2

Summaries
of NORTH AND SOUTH

A general summary

Margaret Hale, the daughter of a minister of the Church of England, returns to her parents' home in the southern village of Helstone, after a long stay in London with her aunt, Mrs Shaw, and her cousin Edith. While in London she has met and become friendly with Henry Lennox, a young lawyer. He is the brother of Captain Lennox, the man whom Edith marries. Henry Lennox pays a visit to Helstone, and proposes to Margaret, who turns down his proposal. On the same day her father informs her that he is giving up his position in the Church for reasons of conscience, and that the family has to move to Milton, an industrial town in the North.

This move is very difficult for all of them, especially for Mrs Hale. Milton is a busy factory town, with smoky chimneys, and inhabitants who are different from the humble villagers of Helstone, and from the sophisticated upper class society she has known in her youth. She finds it difficult to adjust to both the town and its inhabitants.

Mr Hale's attitude is different. He has come to Milton on the recommendation of his friend Mr Bell, an Oxford Fellow, and owner of property in Milton, because he expected to find in this city students to tutor. One of the first to respond to his search for students is Mr John Thornton, a rich and intelligent factory-owner. The two enjoy each other's company and appreciate each other's intellect and different characteristics and backgrounds. Thornton falls in love with Margaret, and is led to believe, by Margaret's behaviour towards him in a critical situation, that she returns his love. He proposes, and is rejected in a manner that hurts his feelings. This critical situation had arisen at a demonstration of workers during a strike which the workers in Milton stage against the mill-owners, and during which Thornton's life seems to be in danger. This rejection of his proposal of course creates a great tension between Thornton and Margaret.

In the meantime Margaret has met Bessy Higgins, the very sick daughter of a workman who is active in the Workers' Union. From him, on the one hand, and from Thornton's conversations with her father, on the other hand, Margaret has learnt a great deal about labour relations in Milton. Higgins is one of the workers who lose their jobs as a result of the strike.

Margaret would like to improve the tense relationship that exists between herself and Thornton, for she values his friendship and would like to win it back, but another incident occurs which makes things worse. Margaret has a brother, Frederick, who years before was involved in a mutiny, and is threatened with court martial and execution if he ever returns to England. Mrs Hale becomes very sick and, knowing that she is going to die, asks Margaret to send for Frederick. He comes secretly, but on the day of his departure, after Mrs Hale's death, Thornton sees Margaret with him at a railway station far from their house. He assumes, of course, that this is her lover. At the same time, a railway porter, who had been a sailor on Frederick's ship, recognises Frederick and wants to report him. Frederick and he have a scuffle, and the porter trips and falls. He dies later, as a result of the fall and the bad state of his health. Margaret is identified as having been present, but she denies everything when the police inspector questions her, because she is not sure that Frederick is safely out of England. Thornton knows about this, and Margaret realises that he must now think of her as a liar.

Not long after these events, Mr Hale dies, and Margaret becomes the ward of Mr Bell, her father's friend. She leaves Milton and returns to her relatives in London. As her material situation improves, Thornton's deteriorates. The strike has affected his business very badly, and soon he realises that he will have to give it up and find employment. He has in the meantime, however, hired Higgins, who has come to him at Margaret's encouragement; and the two of them have managed to influence each other's thinking in such a way, that Thornton's relations with his workers have greatly improved. It is also through Higgins that Thornton finds out that the young man he has seen with Margaret at the station is her brother.

Mr Bell also dies, and leaves Margaret all his property and money. The property includes the premises which Thornton has been renting for his factory all these years; and when he decides to give up his independent business, he comes to London to discuss with her lawyer the possibility of subletting these premises. On this occasion he and Margaret meet again. Margaret offers to lend him the money to continue to run his business independently. But, more important, he realises that he still loves her, and feels that she now returns his love.

So the novel has a happy ending with the marriage of two people who start out so differently from each other, as regards social background, interests, education, but who close this gap through intelligent understanding and love.

Detailed summaries

Chapter 1: 'Haste to the Wedding'

North and South starts with preparations for the wedding of Edith Shaw to Captain Lennox. Among the people we are introduced to on this occasion is the main character of the novel, Margaret Hale, Edith's cousin and daughter of a clergyman, whose living is in Helstone, a small village in the south of England. For the past nine years, since the age of nine, Margaret has been living with her widowed aunt Mrs Shaw and Edith, at 96 Harley Street, London, in surroundings of wealth and comfort. She is now looking forward to returning to her parents' modest home after Edith's wedding. Edith will be accompanying her husband to Corfu, where he is to be stationed; and Mrs Shaw, a kindly but self-centred woman, is planning to take a long holiday in Italy. Among the other characters present is Henry Lennox, the Captain's brother. He is a lawyer who is on friendly terms with Margaret. Before they part he promises to visit her in Helstone.

COMMENTARY: This opening chapter introduces the reader to the Shaw family's home in an elegant street in London. We also get a glimpse of fashionable London society, and the author points out, indirectly, that although these people are kind and generous, they are rather superficial. This setting and these people will form a contrast to Margaret's home and to Margaret herself.

GLOSSARY:

Titania:	Queen of the Fairies, in Shakespeare's *Midsummer Night's Dream*. She is pretty, but not serious
parsonage:	the house of a clergyman, provided by the church
in default of:	in the absence of
mots:	words, from the French; implying witty remarks
Belgravia:	a fashionable London quarter
Sleeping Beauty:	a princess in a fairy tale who slept for one hundred years and was awakened by a prince's kiss

Cinderella:	another fairy tale character, a poor girl whose godmother helps her to go to a ball where she meets a prince whom she marries
green:	a large plot of grass, usually in the centre of a village
living:	a church position, like that of a clergyman, with an income from a special fund

Chapter 2: Roses and Thorns

On her return to Helstone with her father, who had come to attend Edith's wedding, Margaret tries to settle down to the quiet life of a village parsonage. Her greatest pleasure is in the walks she can take when the weather is fine. At the same time she feels a strain at home, expressed in various ways by her mother's dissatisfaction over her father's lack of preferment in the Church, and by her father's preoccupied air, and the fact that he shuts himself up in his study more than usual. Another question which worries Margaret is the mystery which surrounds her brother's absence. Frederick Hale had been involved in a mutiny at sea and had settled in Spain, unable to return to England. He is missed particularly by his mother, and by Dixon, her maid, who never hides her conviction that Mrs Hale's marriage to a poor clergyman had been a mistake. But on the whole, Margaret is satisfied with life, and is on the point of going out sketching one morning, when Mr Henry Lennox is announced.

COMMENTARY: The setting (the place where the events take place) changes. Margaret returns home. Notice the contrast. Also, consider whether Margaret's mother has anything in common with Mrs Shaw, her sister. Frederick is mentioned for the first time. Watch out for his name in future, and see what role he plays in the novel. Another new character is Dixon, Mrs Hale's maid. Servants in middle-class and upper-class Victorian families were usually very loyal, and also snobbish. We are also given a hint of Margaret's snobbish attitude towards people 'in trade', that is, in business.

NOTES AND GLOSSARY:

disparity of age:	difference in age. Mrs Shaw's husband had been much older than she
a silver grey glacé silk:	a dress made of grey silk with a shiny surface (from the French)

a white chip bonnet: bonnets (women's head-coverings) were made of thin strips of wood

Figaro: a character in an opera *The Barber of Seville*, by Beaumarchais (1732-1799). He was the barber, and always in demand

comeliness: good looks

commons: a public or common area in a village or town

dainty messes: soft food, suitable for sick people

preferment: promotion in one's work, particularly in the Church

'he is so thrown away': so wasted, that is, too good for this place

'three learned professions': law, divinity and medicine

backgammon: a game played by two people involving dice and black and white pieces (very popular in Arab countries)

Thomson's Seasons, Hayley's Cowper, Middleton's Cicero: *The Seasons* (1730), 4 blank verse poems by the Scottish poet James Thomson (1700-48); *The life of Cowper* (1803), a biography of the poet William Cowper (1731-1800), by William Hayley (1745-1820), a poet and biographer; *The Life of Cicero,* the Roman orator, statesman and author, by Conyers Middleton (1683-1750) a controversialist

alias: in this context it means 'in other words'

Chapter 3: 'The More Haste the Worse Speed'

To Margaret's surprise, Henry Lennox takes the opportunity of a few minutes privacy to declare his love to her and propose. She has always liked him and looked on him as a good friend. She has never had, nor expected from him, any other feelings, and turns him down. After the first disappointment, he decides not to give up hope of winning her love one day, and with this thought he returns to London.

COMMENTARY: Henry proposes because he loves her, and in spite of the fact that young men in his class tended to look for rich brides. Why can she not return his love? The answer would give a clue to her character. Besides this, we are told that there was a 'strong pride' in her. This is a trait in her character which will be mentioned often again.

NOTES AND GLOSSARY:

'parler du soleil et l'on en voit les rayons': speak of the sun and you see its rays (*French*). Mrs Gaskell likes to use French words and expressions. This comes from her travels in France and her love for it and its people. The English expression is: 'Speak of the devil and he will appear'

chambers in the Temple: the Temple, a district in London in which mainly lawyers have their offices

a brace of carp: 'carp', a freshwater fish; 'a brace of', two of something (Mrs Hale is pleased that she could offer their visitor more than just cold meat)

arrière-pensée: (*French*) mental reservation; something thought, not spoken

beurré: (*French*) a kind of pear

Cockney: native of London

lover: in this novel and in all Victorian fiction this means simply a man who loves the girl and wishes to marry her. The word did not have the connotations that it has in the twentieth century. Keep this in mind, because the word is going to come up often

---

Chapter 4: Doubts and Difficulties

After Henry's departure, and after tea that evening, Mr Hale tells his daughter of the serious decision he has taken which has been weighing on his mind. Finding it impossible to continue to serve the Church of England and to accept all its articles of belief, he has found it necessary, for his conscience's sake, to resign his living, that is, the position he has in his church in Helstone. He has therefore decided to leave Helstone, and to move his family to Milton-Northern, a manufacturing town in the North. Although Margaret is full of prejudice against the North, and anything to do with trade and manufacture, she agrees with her father that Milton will have the advantage of not reminding them of Helstone. In addition, Mr Hale hopes to find tutoring work there to supplement the small income that will be left to them after he resigns his living.

Margaret is left with the unpleasant and difficult duty of breaking this news to her mother.

COMMENTARY: The main point here is Mr Hale's decision to leave the Church of England, and so his position in it. Mrs Gaskell does not make quite clear what his reasons are — but it is clear that they are reasons of conscience. He apparently cannot accept the 'Thirty-nine Articles', which are the thirty-nine statements, basic articles of faith, of the Church of England, and therefore feels it would be dishonest and sinful of him to hide his doubts and remain in the Church. He is still a believing Christian, however.

This act on his part throws much light on his character. It also serves to move the action to another setting. Three more points to note are:

(1) The northern city of Milton (actually Manchester, where Mrs Gaskell lived after her marriage) forms another contrast to Helstone, and also, as we shall see, to London.

(2) It becomes clear that Mr Hale is sure of, and needs, Margaret's strength.

(3) Two characters, Mr Bell and Mr Thornton, who will play important roles later on, are mentioned.

NOTES AND GLOSSARY:

an offer:	in this context, a proposal of marriage
worsted work:	handwork with wool thread
Close:	an enclosed area, like a courtyard, close to a cathedral
Sodom apples:	sometimes also called 'Dead Sea apples' — a legendary fruit which turns to ashes in the mouth, named after Sodom, one of the two cities near the Dead Sea destroyed by God for their wickedness (see the Bible, Genesis 13, 18, and 19). This refers to any disappointing thing; here a wish fulfilled in a way that makes it undesirable
Liturgy:	the prescribed order for worship in churches. Mr Hale is referring to the liturgy in the Church of England which he cannot accept any more
Fellow:	a Fellow at Oxford is a member of the college

Chapter 5: Decision

After the eventful day a miserable night follows for Margaret. Next morning, after her father leaves for the day, Margaret cannot bear the burden of the news any longer, and blurts it out to her mother without any preparation. Mrs Hale's reaction is what we might expect. First she cannot believe it, then she complains because she has not been consulted and informed earlier. She falls sick. Dixon also reacts in a predictable manner, by renewing her veiled criticism of Mr Hale, until Margaret rebukes her very strongly. From this moment on, Dixon's respect for Margaret grows, as she recognises the latter's strong character.

The preparation and plans for moving are left to Margaret, who decides to have her mother and Dixon stay in Heston, a seaside town not far from Milton, while she and her father find a suitable place for them to live in Milton.

COMMENTARY: Besides moving the action slightly forward, this chapter reinforces the impression we have already received of Margaret's strength of character, of her mother's habit of complaining and her somewhat superficial understanding of her husband, and of the rather snobbish attitude both mother and daughter have towards 'trades people'. At this point the reader might ask himself two questions: What do Margaret and her mother have in common? And how do they differ?

NOTES AND GLOSSARY:

red flannel: it was considered good for rheumatism

gruel: a thin porridge; it is often recommended, in nineteenth century novels, to anyone feeling ill

schismatic: someone separated from the church

heretic: someone who disagrees with, and separates from, the accepted teachings of a church (not very different from schismatic)

sceptic: someone who has doubts concerning certain religious principles

'nipped in the bud': wiping out something before it has a chance to grow

'Church and King and down with the Rump': a Cavalier, royalist toast, used in the last years of the reign of Charles I

Dissenter: someone who dissents from, disagrees with, the Established Church, the Church of England (see *Introduction*)

Methodist: a member of the Methodist Church, a movement originally within the Church of England, led by the Wesley brothers (see *Introduction*)

Chapter 6: Farewell

The two weeks left to them in Helstone pass, and on the last day Margaret, hiding her real feelings, quietly and efficiently supervises the final packing, then, after dark, goes for a last walk in the garden. For the first time she feels fear at being alone out of doors after dark. She is glad to return to the house. The next day the family, accompanied by Dixon, leaves Helstone. Their first night's stop is in London, a busy town full of rushing people, who have no time for the sorrowing and the troubled.

COMMENTARY: Again the setting changes. Helstone, the 'South' of Margaret's youth, is left behind. The overnight stop in London emphasises two things:
(1) the contrast between the indifference of Londoners to strangers, and the friendly people in the village;
(2) the contrast between Margaret's present stay in London and the years she spent there at her aunt's house.

NOTES AND GLOSSARY:

to give way:	here it means 'to let her feelings show'
poacher:	one who catches birds, deer, fish, illegally, on someone else's property
Camilla:	a Volscian princess, mentioned in the *Aeneid* of Virgil (70-19 BC), who could run so fast that the grassblades did not bend under her feet

Chapter 7: New Scenes and Faces

Their next stop is Heston, and here Margaret has her first experience with the North. She feels right away that people are busier and more serious here than in seaside towns in the South. Mr Hale and Margaret then go to Milton where, with the help of their new acquaintance, Mr Thornton, they find a suitable house. Mr Thornton is a successful Milton manufacturer who has been introduced to them by Mr Bell, an old friend of Mr Hale.

Margaret's first impression of Milton is of a 'faint taste and smell of smoke' in the air, and of people going about their work busily and purposefully. As for Mr Thornton, she classes him with the tradesmen she looks down upon, but is willing to grant that he is 'sagacious and strong'. She, in turn, has impressed Mr Thornton with her calm beauty, but also with her seeming 'proud indifference'.

COMMENTARY: We have some more contrasts in this chapter: the people of Heston and Milton differ from those of London. They are just as busy, but there seems to be something more honest and genuine about them.

Margaret's attitude towards Mr Thornton is what we have been led to expect. It becomes one of the major themes and tensions in the novel, and will affect her relationship with him. How can her feeling be explained? Test your knowledge of the text by asking yourself how many characters have been introduced in the first seven chapters. What is their relationship with Margaret?

NOTES AND GLOSSARY:

smock-frock: a loose outer garment worn by workers

'unparliamentary' smoke: Parliament had passed a bill in 1853 according to which the factories were to improve their furnaces and chimneys so that there would be less smoke. This remark indicates that Mrs Gaskell is setting the novel in the present

dates from: in this context, writes from, gives as his address

Chapter 8: Home Sickness

It takes Margaret a long time to become reconciled to Milton. There is a thick November fog which threatens her mother's health and reminds her of beautiful Helstone. Then a letter arrives from Edith, describing her gay and carefree life in Corfu, which only emphasises the contrast between her present life and the past. Dixon is also dissatisfied. It is very difficult to find a suitable servant to help her. The girls in Milton are more independent and less awed by Dixon than the simple girls in Helstone; and besides, the cotton mills provide work for many of them.

Margaret gradually gets used to the crowd of workers, men and women, who fill the streets at certain times of the day. She also stops minding the frank way in which they look at her and address her. From among these crowds she gradually singles out a middle-aged, tired looking man, whom she often sees accompanied by a sickly looking young girl. They enter into conversation; she finds out their names and promises to visit them. This one human contact with a father and his daughter makes her feel more friendly towards the whole city.

In the meantime, Mr Hale has found several pupils to tutor, young and not so young men, who, having entered business at an early age, feel the need to make up for a missed education. His favourite among them is Mr Thornton, whom he often praises and quotes to his wife and daughter.

COMMENTARY: Notice the symbolism of the fog, which emphasises the darkness and loneliness of the new life. Notice also that Margaret feels at ease with Higgins and his daughter, although they are socially far beneath her. Why does she not feel the same way towards Thornton, who is much closer to her socially?

It is Higgins who uses the expression 'North and South'. Perhaps his role in the novel will be more significant than the reader expects.

The daughter is suffering from a lung disease brought on by work in the cotton-mills. Consumption, or tuberculosis, was the most common lung disease, and a very common and incurable disease of the nineteenth century. This may really be what Bessy has, though it may have been made worse by work in the cotton mill. Bessy belongs to a fanatically religious group who talk in this strange way about death and heaven. Her dialect will not be difficult to understand.

NOTES AND GLOSSARY:

'sucking situations': easy, elementary work, suitable for training immature ('sucking') young men
Aristides the Just: an Athenian general and statesman (?530-?468 BC) known for being just. It annoyed some people that he was always referred to as 'the Just'
nonpareil: (*French*) having no equal
hoo: (*dialect*) she

(From here on you will encounter many dialect words. All the difficult ones will be explained. Sometimes you will get the meaning if you read the passage out loud.)

Chapter 9: Dressing for Tea

Mr Hale informs his wife and daughter that he has invited Mr Thornton to tea. Neither of them is very pleased, but Margaret, for her father's sake, is willing to do her share of the work to make his visit pleasant.

The scene then moves to the Thorntons' house, and we meet Mrs Thornton, Thornton's mother. Her son comes home and tells her that he is going to have tea with the Hales, and she is even less pleased than Mrs Hale, and warns her son against being caught by 'a penniless girl'. Thornton reassures her that Margaret had treated him with 'a haughty civility which had a strong flavour of contempt in it'. This angers his mother even more, and her last words to herself as the chapter ends are, 'Despise him! I hate her!'

COMMENTARY: This is one the shortest chapters in the novel. It does four things:

(1) It reveals again the varying degrees of contempts with which Margaret and her mother look at tradesmen.
(2) It introduces a new character, Mrs Thornton, and emphasises the difference between her and Mrs Hale.
(3) It prepares the reader for a struggle between Mrs Thornton and Margaret.
(4) It brings up more explicitly the different values held by two different social classes.

NOTES AND GLOSSARY:

querulousness: complaining

ad libitum: (*Latin*) in accordance with his own wishes

clear-starcher: someone who starches, stiffens clothes with starch, a special white substance (here clear, transparent starch) before they are ironed. In the nineteenth century ladies' caps were usually starched

'Pythias to your Damon': Damon and Pythias in Greek legend were two young men living in Syracuse whose friendship was proverbial

'Matthew Henry's Bible Commentaries: a book by a non-Conformist, or Dissenting, minister, Matthew Henry (1662-1714), interpreting the Bible

'morceau de salon': (*French*) a piece of music to be played in a salon; light music, meant to entertain guests and not of a particularly high standard

renegade clergyman: a clergyman who has been a traitor to his church. This is an unfair way of referring to Mr Hale

Chapter 10: Wrought Iron and Gold

This chapter describes Mr Thornton's visit to the Hales. Again we have emphasis on contrasts — here noticed through the eyes of Thornton as he looks around the Hales' drawing-room and contrasts its simplicity and comfort with the expensively furnished rooms in his house which lack comfort. More than anything in the room his admiration focuses of course on Margaret.

Another contrast, or at least difference, is seen through Margaret's eyes as she watches her father and Thornton talk and notices the difference in outward appearance. Her father's face has a gentle, almost feminine beauty, Mr Thornton's has strength and seriousness, with a rare smile which Margaret particulary likes.

The conversation turns on machinery, manufacturing, master-labour relations, and of course the respective merits of North and South, about which Thornton and Margaret argue. Thornton defends the stand of the manufacturers who have become fair in their treatment of the workers, until 'the power of masters and men became more evenly balanced, and now the battle is pretty fairly waged between us'.

Thornton tells them about his own life, to show that all hardworking people can succeed, and to explain why he has no use for 'self-indulgent, sensual people'. When he gets up to leave, Margaret, through an oversight which she immediately regrets, does not take his hand which he has held out for a handshake, and so he leaves, thinking 'A more proud, disagreeable girl I never saw. Even her great beauty is blotted out of one's memory by her scornful ways'.

COMMENTARY: This chapter contains little action and much conversation. Besides revealing character, the conversation introduces the important themes of industrial growth, labour relations, efficiency versus humanitarianism. It also introduces and emphasises new contrasts and tensions, and ends with a comment on Margaret's 'pride'.

When you are revising this chapter you might ask yourself what you think the heading of this chapter is meant to suggest. You may also find it useful to sum up Mr Thornton's views.

NOTES AND GLOSSARY:

taper:	elongated, gradually becoming narrower; here describing Margaret's beautiful arms
steam hammer:	a new kind of machine driven by steam (steam was being used more and more to drive machines)

'Chevy Chase': an old English ballad
mother-wit: natural intelligence
Richard Arkwright: (1732-92)the inventor of the first mechanical spinning frame (1769)
rudiments: basic foundations

Chapter 11: First Impressions

The Hales naturally discuss their visitor after he leaves. Margaret likes his simply told story of his early life, but her mother is not very pleased about having been introduced in her own house to a tradesman whose father had died 'in miserable circumstances'. Mr Hale then adds to this what he had heard from Mr Bell. The father had committed suicide after wild speculations which had left him deep in debt. With his mother's help and support the son had worked hard, repaid the debts, and been taken in as a partner by one of the creditors. Margaret then reveals her prejudice against manufacturers, by exclaiming that it was a pity that such a fine character should be tainted by being a manufacturer. This made him judge everything by money standards. Mr Hale defends him, and they all go to bed. Both father and daughter have noticed, in the meantime, that the mother looks tired, and Margaret, in particular, is more worried than ever about her mother's health.

Next day, on her way to look again for a servant to help Dixon, Margaret meets Bessy Higgins, who confides in her that although she is feeling slightly better, she is looking forward to death: 'longing to get away to the land o' Beulah', as she puts it. She walks with Bessy to Bessy's house, where she meets Bessy's father and sister. The father's tough exterior hides a soft heart, and he cannot hide from Margaret the sorrow he feels over his daughter's failing health. He does not, however, share his daughter's religious convictions.

On returning home Margaret hears that Mrs Thornton is planning to visit them the following day.

COMMENTARY: Margaret is introduced to a working class family.

We realise that one of the novel's conflicts is going to be between Margaret and Thornton: not what he *is*, but what he stands for.

NOTES AND GLOSSARY:
tainted: spotted, slightly spoilt
out of the pale of his sympathies: he had no sympathy with them

Beulah:	a land of rest and quiet near the end of life's journey (from *Pilgrim's Progress* by John Bunyan (1628-88)); in other words, near heaven
wench:	girl
fretted against:	rubbed against; here, protested against
slatternly:	untidy
methodee fancies:	strange Methodist ideas

Chapter 12: Morning Calls

At the insistence of her son, Mrs Thornton visits Mrs Hale and Margaret. She is accompanied by her daughter Fanny who is also going against her will. Fanny has a weak character, and is constantly complaining about feeling tired, and about having a headache. She obviously lacks the strength of character of her mother and brother.

The visit is not a success. It does not have the effect which Thornton hoped for of bringing the four ladies closer to each other. Margaret antagonises Mrs Thornton by honestly expressing her lack of interest in the factories of Milton; and also, through a misunderstanding, manages to offend her.

Neither Mrs Thornton nor Fanny has any intention of repeating this visit.

COMMENTARY: This is another short chapter (similar to the one in which Mr Thornton visits the Hales), mainly to bring out the character differences more sharply, as Margaret and Mrs Thornton confront each other. But they also have something in common, namely pride and honesty.

Notice the 'point of view' in this chapter, the position from which something is considered. We see into Mrs Thornton's mind, and note how she looks at certain people and things, and what she thinks of them. This novel is told in the third person, by an 'omniscient narrator', one who knows everything about everybody, but generally it relates the events from the point of view of Margaret.

NOTES AND GLOSSARY:

Tales of Alhambra:	stories by the American writer Washington Irving (1783-1859). Alhambra is in Spain
killed off:	here it means paid back their visits
unpalatable:	having an unpleasant taste
knick-knacks:	useless but pretty little objects

Chapter 13: A Soft Breeze in a Sultry Place

As soon as Mrs Thornton and her daughter leave, Margaret goes to visit Bessy Higgins. She finds her weaker than the day before. At her request, and to entertain her, Margaret describes Helstone to her, the beautiful countryside, hills, heather, and above all, peace and quiet. Bessy thinks that in a place like that she could rest; and then, referring to her father's lack of religious faith, she expresses a feeling of despair in case it should turn out that her father was right, and there was nothing to look forward to after death.

Bessy also describes to Margaret conditions in the carding-room with the 'fluff', bits of cotton so fine they look like dust, flying around and entering her lungs. Many people working there have suffered from this same lung disease. To Margaret's question if nothing can be done, Bessy answers that there is a method, a great wheel, which can draw the dust away; but most manufacturers are not willing to go to the expense of installing one. Bessy then expresses her worry about her younger sister Mary. She does not want her to go to a factory. Margaret promises to be a friend to her.

Mrs Hale's health is also deteriorating. Margaret looks back on the past year — one year has almost passed since Edith's wedding day — and she realises that taken day by day it has not been so bad, and that in fact it has even had some enjoyment. Her mother, she feels, has changed. She is now gentler and quieter, and more patient than when she had nothing to complain about. When Margaret expresses her worry about her mother's health to her father, he does not want to admit that she is sick. But he finally agrees to call in a doctor.

COMMENTARY: This chapter tells us more about the bad working conditions in most of the factories. We are also prepared for the serious sickness of Mrs Hale.

The time element is emphasised: almost a year has passed since Edith's marriage and the beginning of the events related in the novel. The author often reminds us how much time has passed. The chronology is always clear.

This is a good point at which to review the many changes in Margaret's life, and also the change in her character.

It would be helpful to make a list of all these changes.

NOTES AND GLOSSARY:

rough-stoning: cleaning by rubbing hard with a special stone

flag:	here, stone-tile, used for paving the floor
'to set me up':	to prepare me
carding-room:	the room in the factory where the cotton fibres were cleaned and treated to prepare them for spinning
nesh:	(*dialect*) weak
Book òf Revelations:	the last book in the New Testament, in which St John describes the divine revelations he had while he was living on the Greek island of Patmos. It was originally meant as a call to Christians to resist the threats of the Roman Emperor and to remain strong in their faith. The dangers and rewards are expressed in symbolic language, and have also been taken to mean the rewards awaiting the pious after death or at the Day of Judgement. This is Bessy's favourite book in the Bible

Chapter 14: The Mutiny

Mrs Hale's sickness brings her and her daughter closer together. One evening, when Mr Hale is absent from home, Mrs Hale begins to talk about Frederick, and Margaret finally finds out more about him. Her mother tells her that he had been a naval officer under a very tyrannical captain. There had been a mutiny on board the ship, and Frederick was accused of taking part. Now he is afraid to come back to England, because he will be tried and hanged if he is caught. He is living in Spain, they don't know exactly where, and has changed his name to Dickenson.

COMMENTARY: The punishment for mutiny was very harsh; the reasons are explained to Margaret by her father in Chapter 25. Why do you think Frederick is mentioned now? Consider what role he will play, and whether the story would be very different without him.

NOTES AND GLOSSARY:

Japan cabinet:	a cabinet varnished in the Japanese way
midshipman:	a student naval officer
dirk:	dagger
slaver:	a ship used in the slave trade (the slave trade had been abolished in England and its possessions in 1807)

hindmost: last
cat-o'-nine-tails: a whip made of nine knotted cords

Chapter 15: Masters and Men

Margaret and her father return Mrs Thornton's call. Mrs Hale does not accompany them because she is not feeling well. On the way Mr Hale brings up the subject of his wife's health, and Margaret now insists on calling a doctor. They decide to ask Mrs Thornton to recommend one to them.

The Thorntons live in a large house right near the factory, which makes it very noisy. Everything in the drawing-room, they discover, is expensive, clean, and in its place. But it is not a comfortable room to be in. Margaret tries to explain why her mother has not come, but manages to give the wrong impression to Mrs Thornton, who is offended.

The conversation turns around her son. She does not see why he should read the classics, as a businessman should be spending his time and energy in looking after his business. She is obviously very proud of her son and his achievements. They also speak of the strike that is threatened by the workers. Mrs Thornton is of course on the side of the 'masters', and accuses the workers of struggling for power with the owners. When Margaret expresses some fears of a strike breaking out, Mrs Thornton tells her if she wants to live in Milton, she must be brave.

Later in the evening Mr Thornton comes to visit the Hales and to bring the address of the doctor whom his mother is recommending. The conversation gets around to the threatened strike, and there follows a long conversation about the rights of the workers and of the masters. Mr Thornton's view is that of a strict parent or dictator. He implies that the masters know best, that he himself has set them a good example of honesty, and that, therefore, he expects from his men honesty in return.

Margaret criticises the factory owners. Her criticism is obviously based on something Higgins has told her. She therefore defends the point of view of the workers, who claim that the masters do not want them to get educated.

Mr Hale expresses the view that the workers have now reached the stage of wanting more independence, like children who have become adolescents.

Both Margaret and her father feel that the relationship between masters and men should be better. Margaret emphasises the interdependence of the two groups; they both rely on and need each other. Mr Hale remarks on the fact that the disagreements between the two groups are very apparent even to outsiders.

They part on friendly terms, however. But Margaret does not put out her hand to shake his. He sets this down to pride.

COMMENTARY: This is a long 'talky' chapter: much conversation and little action. There are several things to note:

(1) The description of the Thorntons' drawing-room: in its cleanliness, stiffness, and the wealth it reflects, it represents the character of Mrs Thornton, and emphasises the contrast between the Thorntons and the Hales.

(2) Master-worker relationships: more is revealed here about this important subject, and we notice that Margaret and her father feel the gap between the two groups. We note also that, in spite of herself, Margaret listens to Thornton's explanation.

(3) Use of analogy: Thornton uses two analogies to describe his idea of the role of the master in a. master-worker relationship: (a) a constitutional monarchy growing out of wise despotism, and (b) a strict but just parent.

(4) Thornton is annoyed when Margaret mentions Captain Lennox, whom he knows nothing about. Why?

(5) Mention of Margaret's pride in the last sentence.

NOTES AND GLOSSARY:

lurry:	here, a long flat wagon running on wheels, for transporting goods
drugget:	a rough cloth used for covering the floor
mill:	in this book the word is used to mean 'factory'. 'Mill' was commonly used in this way in the nineteenth century
bagged-up:	protected from dust by being put in a bag
whirligig:	something or someone that continually moves or changes
hedge-lawyers:	poorly trained lawyers, who do their business 'under hedges' or by the roadside
millennium:	literally, a thousand years; a period of great happiness and perfect government which religious people believe will come

Utopia:	an imaginary and ideal country invented and described by Thomas More (1478-1535) in his book *Utopia*, published in 1516. Literally the word means 'nowhere'
Plato's Republic:	the ideal state, as imagined and described by Plato in *The Republic* (4th century BC)
Cromwell:	Oliver Cromwell (1598-1658), leader of the Puritan party which defeated King Charles I and put him to death, was Lord Protector of England from 1653-58. He was known as a strict ruler

Chapter 16: The Shadow of Death

The next day Dr Donaldson calls. Only Dixon is allowed to be present at the examination. But Margaret then stops him on his way out and insists on knowing the truth. The doctor has to admit that the disease is fatal. After Margaret gets over the shock, she decides not to tell her father yet. When she recovers her strength, she goes up to her mother, who realises that, contrary to her wishes, Margaret has found out the truth. She then expresses her great longing to see her son again, and this leads to a violent emotional state. Dixon has to come and help to calm her. The common sorrow draws Margaret and Dixon closer, and they stop seeing each other as rivals for Mrs Hale's love.

At the end of this chapter Dixon sends Margaret out for a walk.

COMMENTARY: The mother's serious illness serves to bring Frederick into the story.

NOTES AND GLOSSARY:

'two short sentences':	this reveals Victorian unwillingness to mention anything unpleasant by proper names. Here we may assume that the mother had cancer
'Nay, my dear young lady':	the doctor apparently refuses payment
Elder Brother:	the older brother in the parable of the Prodigal Son, in the New Testament (Luke 15: 11-32), who demanded his rightful place when the younger, the prodigal brother, was welcomed back by the father
game:	here, brave
jog-trot:	here, a routine habit, referring to the uneventful life Margaret had led in London
ottoman:	an upholstered seat

Chapter 17: What is a Strike?

Margaret leaves the house, intending to go for a long walk that will take her out to the fields. But she finds the streets full of loiterers, men and women. She does not like to walk through these crowds, so instead decides to visit Bessy Higgins.

She finds the father, Nicholas, at home too. And again she becomes involved in a conversation about the strike, this time with someone representing the strikers' point of view. Margaret finds it difficult to understand the problem, as she only has the agricultural world of the South to go by. Nicholas tries to explain that they are striking for a cause; the masters want to reduce their pay rate and they will not accept this. When Margaret suggests that the masters may have a reason for doing this, Nicholas answers, 'We help them make their profits, and we ought to help spend 'em'. This is a well-known slogan.

Among the masters he mentions who will be affected by the strike is Thornton. But he compares him favourably with the others, as he is the only one with whom the fight will be an 'honest up and down fight'.

Bessy then complains that his tobacco smoke makes her choke, and he goes out to finish his pipe. Bessy immediately regrets this, because she fears he may meet some friends who will take him to drink. When Margaret asks if he drinks, Bessy defends him, and says he does so only occasionally, and he can certainly be forgiven, because life is often difficult for him. When she later says that Margaret does not understand suffering, Margaret tells her of her worry about her mother's illness, and her brother's fate. Before she leaves she promises to come back and read her some chapters from the Bible, but not the prophecies, or Revelations, from which Bessy is always quoting.

COMMENTARY: There is a change in Margaret's attitude to the South; she can see it more objectively now. She is also willing to listen to more views on the strike, and tries to bring forward the view of the masters. You will find it useful to summarise in your own words Higgins's views on the strike.

NOTES AND GLOSSARY:

dang:	(*dialect*) damn
welly:	(*dialect*) almost
clemmed:	(*dialect*) starved

workhouse:	a house established to provide work for the poor; living conditions were often very bad and almost prison-like
bate:	reduce
bug-a-boo:	an imaginary object that is frightening
'my latter days':	my last days (Bessy knows she is dying)
be farred:	(*dialect*) be kept at a distance
fillip:	something exciting
four-pounder:	a loaf of bread weighing four pounds
spreeing:	act irresponsibly or without restraints for a while ('going on a spree')
Wormwood:	this quotation is from Revelations 8:11, Bessy's favourite book in the Bible. Wormwood is a plant with a bitter taste. It may also mean 'bitterness' in a figurative sense
deaved:	(*dialect*) worried, tired
fustian:	a strong cotton and linen fabric

Chapter 18: Likes and Dislikes

Upon returning home, Margaret finds an invitation to dinner for her parents and herself from Mrs Thornton. Her mother insists that Margaret and her father should accept the invitation. Margaret does not want her father to suspect yet how seriously sick the mother is, so she gives in.

The scene then shifts to the Thorntons' house and the conversation there centres around two topics: the Hale family, and the strike. Mr Thornton again defends the Hales, especially Margaret. He does not show his mother that he is hurt when she agrees that Margaret would not consider a marriage proposal from him (she is referring to the conversation she had with her at the Hales' house earlier).

The conversation then moves on to the question of the strike. In one of the factories the workers have already gone on strike. Thornton deplores the stupidity — as he sees it — of the strikers, and says that they do not understand the situation. At this time, in order to compete with American yarn on the market, they will have to lower their prices, not raise them, as they would have to do if they raised their wages. He wishes the 'combination laws' were still in force to prevent ignorant men from getting together and acquiring so much power. But he is determined not to give in, even if it means bringing in other workers, from the Spinners' Union, or from Ireland, which might cause more trouble.

COMMENTARY: Note: (1) Mrs Gaskell is usually very careful about time: 'that evening', 'that night', etc.; (2) the 'point of view' changes.

NOTES AND GLOSSARY:

Quakers: a nickname which has stuck, given to the members of the Religious Society of Friends, a Christian group founded by George Fox (1624-91) which broke away from the Established Church in the seventeenth century in protest against the domination of the Church by the State

'rouge you up': bring a red colour to your cheeks

Lyceum: the name given to many institutions in England in the nineteenth century in which lectures on literary and artistic subjects were given

ecclesiastical architecture: church architecture

saucy: bold, impudent

jade: flirtatious girl

Jezebel: a wicked queen in the Old Testament, wife of King Ahab (I Kings, 16, 31, 19; 2 Kings, 9)

cowed: intimidated, frightened

hands: here, workers

turned out: here, gone on strike

Combination laws: laws forbidding the workers to combine into Unions to demand higher wages, or to go on strike. They had been passed in 1799 and had since been repealed, that is, removed

---

Chapter 19: Angel Visits

As the day for the dinner at the Thorntons comes nearer, Mrs Hale shows a great interest in what Margaret is going to wear on that occasion. Margaret has several beautiful dresses from her London days, and she models them all for her mother.

That same day she visits Bessy. When Bessy hears that Margaret is invited to the Thorntons for dinner, she is quite surprised, because, as she says, all the 'first folk' in Milton visit them. Margaret understands her surprise and explains to her that educated people, even when poor, are not inferior to the rich. She also assures Bessy that they can invite

Mr Thornton back, and that she has something suitable to wear to the dinner, a white silk dress. On hearing this, Bessy says she wishes she could see Margaret in it, and then she adds that, before she had even met Margaret, she had dreamt of her, as an angel.

Of course the conversation turns to the strike, and Margaret finds out that Nicholas has gone on strike, along with many others, all of them working for a man called Hamper. Bessy knows a lot about the misery of the strikers and their families, the hatred they feel for their masters, and their conviction that these men have made high profits which they, the workers, should share. Just then Nicholas comes in, and confirms that the workers are ready to fight, and that they are sure of winning.

The one bright spot in the lives of the Hales at the moment is that Mrs Hale seems to be getting better. The doctor's medicines are evidently helping.

At this time Mr Hale is also drawn into conversations about the strike. He hears some of the workers' complaints from acquaintances of his among them, and then he tries to get Mr Thornton's views. Mr Thornton explains everything in economic terms, showing that in trade it is inevitable that some should succeed and others fail, among the masters and the workers. This means that the risk exists for both classes, which means him too. Margaret finds his explanation very hard-hearted and inhuman. She also resents the help he offers for anything her mother needs. This is because she does not want him to be part of what should be, in her opinion, strictly a family secret. At the same time she sees his kindness and pity, and cannot reconcile it with the hard logical way in which he talks about the workers and the strike.

On the day of the Thorntons' dinner, Margaret is very much affected when she visits Bessy and meets there a worker called Boucher. Boucher is not as good or efficient a workman as Higgins. He has a large family and a wife who herself is quite lazy. But his case is really tragic. His wife is dying, and the children slowly starving. He does not trust the Union's wisdom, because so far the employers have not given in, and the workers are beginning to starve. Nicholas defends the Union and promises to help the Bouchers. Before she leaves, Margaret gives Bessy the money she has to buy food for the Bouchers.

COMMENTARY: A new character, Boucher, is introduced, to show us the tragic side of the strike, and also to reveal the power of the Union.

Watch out in the next chapters to see how Boucher's actions affect the course of events. What can you tell about his character from what he says? Compare and contrast him with Higgins.

NOTES AND GLOSSARY:

shining raiment: shining clothes (usually applied to the clothing of angels)

'some's pre-elected': some are chosen ahead of time; that is, God has already chosen ('elected') those to whom he wants to grant salvation

Lazarus: a poor man in a parable in the New Testament (Luke xvi, 20) who suffered in this life, but was rewarded in the next

plaining: (*dialect*) complaining

'give yo' a bumper': give you a toast, that is, to drink to someone's health

'defied the raven': the 'croaking' (used in the previous sentence) of the raven was considered a bad omen. Margaret does not want to believe in it, and does not want to give up hope that her mother will recover

exoteric: outsider

squab: a couch, or a cushion for a chair

cranky: here, (*dialect*) sickly, in poor health

Chapter 20: Men and Gentlemen

On returning home after this visit, Margaret tells her mother about the Boucher family, and Mrs Hale insists on sending them some food that very night. Then she wonders if she has done the right thing, because she has heard Mr Thornton say that any help given the strikers would only prolong the strike, and add to the workers' misery. But Mr Hale assures her that that that was the only thing she could have done, and promises to visit the Bouchers himself next day, which he does. This visit makes him realise that one cannot judge Milton conditions by the same standards as Helstone conditions.

Later that evening at the Thorntons' dinner, Margaret makes a great impression with her beauty and elegance. Mr Thornton is very conscious of her presence, although he hardly looks at her or talks to her. He is, however, aware of the fact that this is the first time he has shaken hands with her. Margaret enjoys listening to the conversation of the men, and she is also impressed by the dignified manner in which

Mr Thornton entertains his guests. She is surprised to notice how much she is enjoying herself, and also to realise that the conversation of the men here is more interesting than that at London parties. She liked the way the men here talked with enthusiasm, even with boastfulness, and she could see the power of this tradesman class.

In a short conversation after dinner she and Thornton get into a discussion about the term 'gentleman', and what it means. Thornton prefers the term 'man', as being more inclusive. Before they can finish this discussion, he is called away by some of the men, and she realises that the conversation has turned to the strike again. Thornton is confident that the struggle with his men will be a clean one.

COMMENTARY: We note that Thornton and Margaret are more conscious of each other as man and woman: he is aware of her physical presence; she admires the strength and assurance in him.

A new contrast is set before us: the men of Milton are contrasted, to their advantage, with the men of London.

The discussion between Thornton and Margaret about the meaning of the word 'gentleman' should also be kept in mind. The Victorians thought much about this. For example, Cardinal Newman (1801-90) wrote a long essay on the subject; and in Charles Dickens's novel *Great Expectations* (1860-1) it is one of the main themes. 'Gentleman' had nothing to do with money, and this is probably why Margaret finds it difficult to admit that a 'tradesman' can also be a gentleman.

Look up a definition of 'gentleman' in a good dictionary, and then write a paragraph giving your own definition of the word.

NOTES AND GLOSSARY:

turn-out: here, one who has gone on strike

Infirmary order: this would gain her admission to a free clinic run for the poor

A Saint in Patmos: the reference is to St. John, who, while on the island of Patmos, had a vision, which he described in the Book of Revelations, the last book of the Bible

---

Chapter 21: The Dark Night

On the way home after the dinner, Mr Hale and Margaret talk about Mr Thornton. Margaret admits that she admires him but she says she finds him unfeeling. She is, however, prepared to like the manufacturing class which he represents. She has enjoyed the talk of the men much more than that of the women, who had tried hard to impress each other with their wealth. When they arrive at home, they are met by Dixon with the shocking news that Mrs Hale has been taken very ill in their absence, and that the doctor has been called. Mr Hale finally realises with a shock that his wife is incurably sick. Watching by the bedside of her sleeping mother, Margaret thinks how vain life really is — 'All are shadows! — All are passing'.

Three days later, the doctor recommends a water-bed which would make her lie more comfortably, and which he is sure Mrs Thornton would be willing to lend them. Margaret starts out for the Thorntons' to ask for it.

When she approaches Marlborough Street, where the Thorntons live next to their factory, even her preoccupied mind becomes aware of the restless crowds in the streets, and the many people gathering round doors and windows. While the careful gateman admits her into the Marlborough mill-yard, and she goes up the steps to the Thorntons' front door, the crowd of people begins to flow into the street.

COMMENTARY: This chapter brings us closer to three crises:
(1) the death of Mrs Hale;
(2) the confrontation between Mr Thornton and the workers;
(3) the critical encounter between Thornton and Margaret.
The second and third points are closely related and will be described in the next chapter.

NOTES AND GLOSSARY:
Leezie Lindsay: a character in an old song
'my first olive': something one is not used to; the second one will taste better
'husbanding resources': here, saving one's strength for later need

---

Chapter 22: A Blow and its Consequences

Margaret arrives at a very bad moment. While she is talking to Mrs Thornton, the crowd has reached the gates and is trying to force its way in. Mrs Thornton sends Fanny to call her son. Fanny has just had time to explain to Margaret that the crowd is angry because her brother has brought workers in from Ireland to replace his striking men, and that these Irish workers were now terrified by the threats of the strikers. Now Mr Thornton comes from the factory and walks into the house, ready to defy the workers. Margaret realises that she herself is not frightened, and that she is not a coward as she had feared she would be. Mr Thornton has sent for the army, but they would not be there for another twenty minutes. In the meantime the crowd is attacking the gates, and finally succeeds in breaking them down and approaching the house. Margaret recognises Boucher in the crowd, mad with rage. When she points him out to Thornton, and Thornton comes closer to the window, the angry people see him and shout for him.

The crowd then turns to the mill-door. That is where the frightened Irish workers are hiding. Margaret then challenges Thornton to go down and speak to the workmen, instead of letting the soldiers come in and cut them down. He accepts her challenge, and asks her to go down with him so that she can bar the door behind him. She does this, and goes back upstairs to watch. She does not see him, as he is right below her, but she sees the crowd's reaction to him. She realises that he has not succeeded in quieting them down, and that they are getting wilder and wilder; and then she notices some young men taking off their clogs, ready to hurl at him. At this she rushes down, unbolts the door, and steps in front of Thornton. She begs them to go away, and tells them that the soldiers may be coming any minute.

Someone in the crowd asks if the Irish workers will be sent away. When Thornton says no, the crowd goes wild. Margaret realises that any moment now one of these clogs will hit Thornton, and the only thing she can think of doing to protect him is to throw her arms around him. But this does not prevent the crowd from trying to attack him. A clog is thrown at him but misses him. Then a stone is thrown which grazes her forehead and makes it bleed. She faints on his shoulder. Then, while he holds her in his arms, he addresses the crowd, criticising them for coming to throw out the innocent strangers (the Irish workers), and then for attacking a woman. The men in the crowd are startled by the blood on Margaret's face, and begin to leave, when one of them calls out to Thornton that the stone was meant for him, but that he had been hiding behind a woman. At these words, Thornton places Margaret on the door-step, walks down the steps, and stands facing the crowd, challenging them to kill him. They leave slowly.

He turns to Margaret, who tries to get up without his help, only to faint again. He carries her into the house, and as he looks at her white face he realises fully how much she means to him. While Mrs

Thornton goes to call a doctor, two of the maids describe to Fanny how Margaret had been hurt. Margaret comes out of her faint in time to hear them say that she had been so bold as to hug Mr Thornton in front of the crowd, and Fanny makes things worse by saying it was obvious that Margaret cared for her brother, but that of course he would never marry her.

All this upsets Margaret so much that she insists on leaving as soon as the doctor arrives with Mrs Thornton, and she is able to sit up.

COMMENTARY: This is one of the crucial chapters in the book. On one level, it describes the incidents which lead to the breakdown of the strike, and so to the defeat of the Workers' Union. On another equally important level, it describes the first physical, one can say sexual, encounter between Thornton and Margaret. Mrs Gaskell uses the rage and the passion of the workers (notice how often she uses the words 'passion' and 'rage', and words with similar meanings), to suggest the feeling of passion that Thornton (consciously) and Margaret (unconsciously) feel for each other. But this is a Victorian novel, and nothing more can happen than that the heroine faints in the hero's arms.

But the author is not yet ready for a 'happy ending.' There are many problems to be solved, and many extremes brought together, including significant differences between the two main characters. The last few pages in this chapter, the conversation of Fanny and the maids, add to the delay of the solutions.

For revision purposes you may find it helpful to describe in your own words the mood of the crowd.

Describe the action and feelings of Margaret from the moment she challenged Thornton to go down and face the workers, to the end of the chapter.

NOTES AND GLOSSARY:

clog:	shoe with a wooden sole, or made entirely of wood
blackguard:	scoundrel, a bad person
retrograde:	backward, retreating

Chapter 23: Mistakes

Mr Thornton returns to find that Margaret has just left. His mother assures him that she was feeling well, and that she was sent home in a cab. Thornton tells his mother about the arrangements he has made to prevent a recurrence of the day's events, but both of them have

Margaret on their mind. Thornton wants to go and ask about her, but Mrs Thornton begs him to put off his visit till the next day. She knows that her son wants to propose to Margaret, and although she does not like her and does not want to share her son with anyone, she encourages him to think that Margaret will accept his proposal.

On Margaret's return home she tells her mother that Mrs Thornton would send the waterbed. She says nothing about the riot or her wound. When she is alone her thoughts go back to the talk she had overheard between the maids and Fanny. She feels a sense of shame that they should so misjudge her action, and that so many people had seen her throw her arms around Mr Thornton. It is clear from the thoughts that turn and torture her that she is not aware of the feelings she has at that moment for Mr Thornton.

COMMENTARY: The modern reader cannot quite understand Margaret's feelings of shame when she remembers the scene with Mr Thornton. But of course they are typical of the Victorian sense of modesty. At the same time, Mrs Gaskell seems to be saying that Margaret is not aware of her real feelings for Mr Thornton.

Try to express these feelings in your own words.

Chapter 24: Mistakes Cleared Up

Next morning Mr Thornton calls on Margaret. He starts out by thanking her for what she had done the day before, then goes on to declare his love for her. Margaret rejects his words and declares that he has offended her, going on to say that no gentleman would have misunderstood her act of the day before. She tells him that she would have done what she did for any man in the crowd. Thornton replies that a man has the right to express his feelings. These are obvious references to the conversation they had at his house on the day of the dinner. They both say sharp things to each other, and finally Thornton tells her that she cannot stop him from loving her, even though it tainted her to be loved by him.

He does not respond to her conciliatory words and leaves. Margaret is left in confusion. She assures herself that she does not really like him, but that she would repeat the same action again, no matter what its consequences.

COMMENTARY: Note the following:
(1) the use of the word 'proud', often applied to Margaret

(2) the use of the word 'tainted' by Thornton. It echoes Margaret's use of it in Chapter 11, when she spoke of Mr Thornton being 'tainted' by his position as a Milton manufacturer.

(3) the irony in the chapter heading, especially when the heading is seen as a continuation of the previous chapter heading. Have you paid attention to chapter headings before this? What does this irony consist of? Explain in one or two paragraphs.

Chapter 25: Frederick

Margaret cannot help comparing the two proposals she has received so far, from Henry Lennox, and now from John Thornton. Henry Lennox she had always considered a friend; and she had regretted that his feelings had gone beyond the limits of friendship. With Mr Thornton it is different. Their acquaintance has been one series of disagreements, and now suddenly he has declared his love; and with a flash it comes upon her that he does love her. This is a strange knowledge, and it seems as if she is frightened by it. Her thoughts finally become unbearable, and she decides to go and visit Bessy Higgins.

She finds Bessy feeling worse, and then discovers that Nicholas is very disturbed by the riot at Marlborough Mills the day before. The Committee, of which he is a member, had decided that no force was to be used at any time, because they wanted their case to remain clear, but Boucher had gone against the will of the Committee and had led the riot. Nicholas had threatened to hand him over to the police, upon which Boucher had hit him and run off. Nicholas assures Bessy that he had no intention of reporting Boucher. Margaret reads to Bessy from the Bible, and when Bessy falls asleep, Margaret returns home.

She finds her mother in the drawing-room, feeling better and rested. She praises the waterbed which Mrs Thornton had lent her, declaring she had not slept in such a comfortable bed since she had left the home of Sir John Beresford, her guardian. This leads to a reference to Frederick. Mrs Hale again expresses her longing to see her son, and begs Margaret to let her see him before she dies. She urges and pleads and says that she cannot even pray until she has seen him. Margaret wants to wait until her father comes home, but her mother is afraid that they would miss the day's mail. So Margaret writes and goes out to mail the letter. On the way back she meets her father. She tells him what she has done. Mr Hale is serious. He tells her what dangers face

Frederick if he comes back and is caught. But then he assures Margaret that she has done the right thing. He would not, however, have dared to do it himself.

COMMENTARY: This chapter makes some important points:
(1) Margaret's feelings for Thornton; they are still unclear to her. What does the author mean by 'She disliked him the more for having mastered her will'?
(2) Higgins's view of the workers' riot the day before. What does it reveal about his character?
(3) Mrs Hale's 'special' feelings for Frederick, and her seemingly selfish love. Do they reveal anything about her character?

NOTES AND GLOSSARY:

'*Fais ce que dois, advienne que pourra*': *(French)* Do your duty come what may

m'appen: *(dialect)* it may happen, perhaps

again: *(dialect)* against

knobstick: one who works during the strike, considered a traitor by the strikers (the modern word is 'scab')

'New Heavens and the New Earth': described in the Book of Revelations, Chapter 21. Bessy, like many Christians, sees this as the promise of a better life after death

---

Chapter 26: Mother and Son

We return to the Thorntons. Mr Thornton leaves Margaret, feeling physical pain at his rejection. He tells himself that he hates her, but keeps coming back to the knowledge that he loves her. Even a long ride into the country, and a chance to think about the whole scene in detail, only bring him back to the conviction that he loves her, and that she can do nothing to stop him.

In the meantime his mother is waiting impatiently for his return. She does not doubt that Margaret will accept him. She cannot think that any girl would refuse a proposal from her son. She is trying to accept the fact that from now on she will have to take second place in her son's love.

When she learns that he has been refused, her jealousy turns to hatred for Margaret. She expresses this very strongly to her son, who answers that this only makes him love her more. He then asks his mother not to refer to the subject again.

After an interval he tells her that warrants were out for three men sought for conspiracy, and that yesterday's riot had helped to end the strike.

COMMENTARY: We can notice here mainly:
(1) Thornton's feelings for Margaret;
(2) Mrs Thornton's feelings for and her relationship with her son. Compare this with the other mother-son relationship in the novel, that of Mrs Hale and Frederick.

NOTES AND GLOSSARY:

fish-wife: a loud-voiced, vulgar woman

omnibus: a vehicle, here of course a carriage, designed to carry many people

magistrate: a man entrusted with the enforcement of the law (*not* a policeman)

his brother magistrates: his colleagues, the other magistrates

warrant: a legal order authorising an officer to make an arrest

conspiracy: a plot, an agreement to carry out an act (usually something against the law)

Chapter 27: Fruit-Piece

Mr Thornton carries on his work as usual the next day. There is business to be settled resulting from the strike and the riot, and everyone depends on him to settle the problems. Even older and richer men rely on his judgement. For a while it is as if his feeling of power and importance has made him forget Margaret, but the feeling comes back, and he walks along the street so deep in thought about her, that he does not see Dr Donaldson, who stops him and talks to him. He mentions Mrs Hale, and tells him that she may not have many more weeks to live. When Mr Thornton asks him if there is anything he can do for her, the doctor suggests that fruit might be a refreshing gift.

Thornton buys a basket of carefully chosen fruit, and carries it over himself, but stays only for a moment, quite ignoring Margaret's presence in the room. The parents comment on Thornton's kindness, and Margaret agrees in her heart, but says little. She then goes to her room to give vent to her feelings, and finds Dixon there, looking for something in the drawers. Dixon tells her that Bessy has died, and that her sister has brought the news, and has asked for something belonging to Margaret that Bessy might be buried in. This was what Bessy had requested. Bessy's sister asks Margaret if she would come and see Bessy laid out, and Margaret promises to do so.

COMMENTARY: Bessy's death is the first of several deaths in this novel. Victorian novels usually contain more than one death. But of course, there were more incurable diseases then, and life expectancy was much shorter than it is now.

NOTES AND GLOSSARY:

lavender:	a plant whose flower has a nice smell. It is often dried and placed among clean clothes to keep them smelling sweet
laid out:	prepared for burial

Chapter 28: Comfort in Sorrow

Margaret goes to the Higginses' house that afternoon to pay her last respects to Bessy. Bessy's calm face, peaceful in death, gives Margaret some calm in her heart. As she prepares to leave she sees Nicholas who has just returned home and heard the news of his daughter's death. He has been out arguing with the Committee members. In his great despair at Bessy's death he turns to leave and go out to drink. Margaret finally persuades him to go home with her. This is the only way she can stop him from getting drunk. Nicholas is not a habitual drunkard, but he drinks to forget his sorrows.

He and Mr Hale get on quite well, and their conversation touches on religion and faith. Nicholas expresses difficulty in believing in something he cannot see. But although he does not believe in another life, he wants to believe in God.

They then talk about the strike. It is obvious that the workmen have made mistakes, just like the masters. They had forgotten that human beings had feelings and weaknesses, and so had not expected some of them to lose control over themselves. The reference here is to the rioters, who have brought the strike to an end, and have blackened the cause of the strikers. Most workers will be ready to go back to work, but Nicholas does not expect to be taken back by Hamper. Hamper considers Nicholas a trouble-maker. More talk follows about labour, capital, strikes, and wages finding their own level. Higgins complains that the masters don't talk to the men civilly, and Hale says he wishes he and Mr Thornton could exchange views. But Higgins criticises Thornton because Thornton had refused to punish the rioters. Thornton felt it would be punishment enough for them if they could not find work, and Higgins had wanted them to be punished to clear the name of the Union. He then tells Margaret what happens to workers who don't join the Union, and she finds that as tyrannical as the behaviour of the masters. But Higgins says it is all the fault of the masters.

Before Higgins gets up to leave, Hale asks him to join them in a family prayer. And so the three, so different from each other, kneel and pray together.

COMMENTARY: This chapter describes Margaret's first encounter with death, to prepare her, and the reader, for her mother's death. It also introduces more ideas about labour, capital, and wages, and brings together for the first time Mr Hale and Higgins. You should notice Mrs Gaskell's views on religion. She herself belonged to the Unitarian Church, which was very liberal in its views. We see here that Mrs Gaskell judges a person by his relationship with God and his fellow-beings, not by the church or sect he belongs to.

Describe in your own words how Union members 'punish' workers who do not join the Union.

NOTES AND GLOSSARY:

gait:	here, way
bed-fast:	sick in bed
dunder-headed:	stupid
'who ossed to treat me':	*(dialect)* who offered to buy me a drink
'without shilly-shallying':	without wasting time by indecision
Daniel O'Rourke:	character in an Irish folk tale who arrived on the moon and refused to leave
'put it in yo'r pipe, and smoke it':	think about it
noddies:	fools
dreed:	*(dialect)* suffered
welly:	*(dialect)* almost
brossen:	*(dialect)* broken
noodle:	here, a stupid person
gibberish:	meaningless language
bolus:	a large pill, a soft mass of chewed food, a lump of earth; here Nicholas probably means Hamper's final word
Churchwoman:	a woman who belongs to the church

Chapter 29: A Ray of Sunshine

Margaret receives a cheerful letter from Edith, who writes about her new baby son, and insists that Margaret and her mother should visit them. She promises that Mrs Hale will recover in that sunny climate.

Mrs Hale has two other things on her mind. She wants to see Mrs Thornton, and she is beginning to worry that something will happen to Frederick if he should come to England. Margaret reassures her.

In the meantime, Mr Thornton continues his visits to the Hales, always treating Margaret with great reserve, although Margaret tries to remove the barrier between them. Both of them are conscious of each other's presence, but not conscious of their feelings for each other. Mrs Hale tells Thornton that she would like to see his mother.

COMMENTARY: The main interest in this short chapter lies in the feelings of Thornton and Margaret. How would you describe these feelings? We also notice again the great contrast between Edith and Margaret, and then between their respective lives.

Read again the last four words, 'as I have said.' This is one of the few times that the author intrudes into the narrative: she leaves the third person method of narration, the 'omniscient narrator,' and says something in her own voice, or in the first person. This is called 'authorial comment.'

NOTES AND GLOSSARY:

Peace Society: a society which held International Peace Congresses in the mid-nineteenth century. Their object was to try and prevent war, partly by refusing to fight

'descended from King Herod': King Herod was the wicked king in the New Testament who had all the children under two killed. Edith means that she would consider Margaret a hater of children. She is of course joking

'slack of work':   without enough work

bugbear: an imaginary object used to excite fear

Chapter 30: Home at Last

Next morning Mrs Thornton comes and visits Mrs Hale. Mrs Hale begs her to be a friend to Margaret. Mrs Thornton reluctantly promises to do so. But as she does not like Margaret, she promises to be a true friend, not a 'tender friend'.

While the visit is taking place, Dixon and Margaret decide that, for Frederick's greater safety, they should send Martha, the servant, away for a holiday. Mary Higgins, Bessy's sister, could help out in her place.

That same afternoon Frederick arrives. There is joy in the midst of sadness when brother and sister meet. They have not seen each other for seven or eight years; but they are drawn to each other immediately, and Margaret feels the strength that his presence gives her in the midst of her sadness. The father and Dixon are also greatly affected by this meeting. All three are of course aware of the danger Frederick is in. Mrs Hale is so calm and happy in the presence of her son, that he finds it difficult to believe the doctor's warning that she may die any time.

Everyone feels Frederick's strong and cheering presence in the house. But the following evening Mrs Hale has convulsions, and becomes unconscious. She dies before morning. Margaret has to gather all her strength, because even Frederick, with his practical theories about life, at last breaks down.

COMMENTARY: Frederick finally arrives. How would you describe his character?

NOTES AND GLOSSARY:

Roman daughter:	strong of character, as the Romans reputedly were
carpet-bag:	a travelling bag originally made of carpet
taper:	here, a kind of thin candle, giving a weak light, used to light a lamp or a fire
lucifer matches:	the forerunner of to-day's 'safety match': a thin piece of wood with a tip of inflammable material which lights when rubbed on a rough surface
'Poeta nascitur, non fit':	(*Latin*) A poet is born, not made
quarter-deck:	the back part of the upper deck in a ship, often used for ceremonies

---

Chapter 31: 'Should Auld Acquaintance be Forgot'

The next day it falls to Margaret to speak about funeral arrangements, since neither Mr Hale nor Frederick is calm enough to do so. Finally Mr Hale suggests that they should ask his friend, Mr Bell in Oxford, and Margaret promises to write to him.

In the meantime, Dixon has had an accidental meeting in the street with a man called Leonards, who had been on the same ship as Frederick, and who knew of Frederick's involvement in the mutiny. Dixon makes the mistake of addressing him. He recognises her and tells her that there is a reward for anyone who can catch Frederick, and that Frederick would be hanged if he ever came back to England. Leonards is a good-for-nothing young man, and Dixon speaks to him rather sharply. He then offers to share the reward with her if she helps him to catch Frederick. Dixon has fortunately not told him that the Hales are living in Milton, but she is very worried and tells Mr Hale that Frederick is in danger.

It is clear that Frederick must leave as soon as possible. Margaret tells him about Leonards, and he remarks that Leonards was really a bad man who betrayed the men to the captain. He mentions then that he had almost been seen by a caller that day, whom he had taken for a shopman. When Margaret finds out that the caller was Mr Thornton, who had come to offer his assistance to her father, she tells her brother that he is a gentleman, and then adds that he is a 'very kind friend'.

In the short time that is left to them, Frederick tells them that he is engaged to marry a girl called Dolores Barbour, who lives in Spain. He hesitantly tells them that she is a Catholic, and that he himself has turned Catholic.

Margaret now urges him, for Dolores' sake, to try and clear himself in court, but Frederick knows that a court-martial would never clear him, even if he could get enough witnesses. They would only consider that he had disobeyed authority, and would not take his motives into account. Margaret then suggests that he should see a lawyer, and she writes a note and sends it with him to Mr Lennox in London, whom he promises to consult on his way back to Spain.

COMMENTARY:

(1) The part of the plot involving Frederick becomes more complicated, with the meeting between Leonards and Dixon.

(2) Frederick's fiancee is a Roman Catholic. This is probably intentional on Mrs Gaskell's part, so that she can extend her religious tolerance to include Roman Catholicism (see the ending of Chapter 28).

(3) Margaret calls Thornton a 'gentleman'.Compare this with her earlier remarks, and see how much she has changed.

(4) Note the weather. It is the same as it was when they first came to Milton, about a year ago.

NOTES AND GLOSSARY:
groom's-man: a male friend who attends the bridegroom at the wedding
chaff: teasing
to curry favour: to try to gain favour by flattery
'au pied de la lettre': (*French*) literally, word for word

Chapter 32: Mischances

Next day Frederick leaves. Margaret accompanies him to the station. They are early, and while they are waiting for the booking office to open, and are standing together with Frederick holding his sister's hand, Mr Thornton passes on horseback. He sees them and greets Margaret very stiffly. They then go in and get the tickets, and just as the train approaches, a railway porter, whom Frederick recognises as Leonards, comes up to them and seizes Frederick by the collar. Frederick trips him up, and he falls. Frederick runs to catch his train, and Margaret is left alone. She is sick and faint after this incident, and decides not to walk home, but to take the train to a station nearer her home. When she goes in to get her ticket she overhears some railway officials talking about Leonards, that he has been drinking again, and that he had just come in and told them about a fall he had had, and that he wanted to borrow money to go to London. But nobody had lent him any money, and he had walked away. Margaret is relieved when her train comes and she gets on it.

COMMENTARY: This short chapter contains two coincidences which are connected, and which will complicate the plot further:
(1) the meeting with Leonards at the station;
(2) the fact that Thornton sees Margaret with a young man whom he does not know.

Chapter 33: Peace

When Margaret returns home she does not tell her father about the incident at the railway station. They speak about their hope of hearing from Mr Bell the next day, and Mr Hale says that if he does not come, he will ask Mr Thornton to go with him to the funeral, as he cannot go alone. Margaret insists that she will go, although it is not customary for women to go to funerals. She says that she does not want strangers at her mother's funeral. Mr Bell cannot come, as he has the gout. However, he hopes to visit them soon.

The night before the funeral a note comes from Mrs Thornton saying that their carriage would attend the funeral. Margaret is upset at the formality, and that Mr Thornton has not offered to go to the funeral. She bursts out crying and her father cannot understand why. The next day she receives a letter from Frederick informing her that Mr Lennox was not in London, and that he intended to remain in London a day or two until Mr Lennox returned. This adds to Margaret's worry.

Margaret needs all her strength to support her father at the funeral. She notices that Nicholas Higgins and his daughter are present, but does not see Mr Thornton, who is also there, and who then asks Dixon how they are. He misinterprets Dixon's words that Margaret is bearing up better than her father. He is sure it must be because of the man he saw her with at the station, who, he assumes, must be her lover. He cannot forget the sight of the two of them, Margaret and Frederick, whom he of course does not know. Margaret never finds out that he was at the funeral.

NOTES AND GLOSSARY:

gout: a painful disease of the joints

carriages at the funeral: it was common to send one's carriage to a funeral instead of going oneself, when the dead person was not a close friend

crape draperies: black coverings; heavy mourning was common in the nineteenth century, especially at the funeral

Charybdis of passion: in classical mythology, Charybdis was a whirlpool off the Sicilian coast; 'Charybdis of passion' is therefore a violent passion

lover: remember, this only means the man who loves her and is courting her

Chapter 34: False and True

Margaret and her father are quite concerned that there is no news from Frederick. It is a relief to both of them when Mr Thornton calls. While he is visiting them, Dixon calls Margaret to the study where a police-inspector is waiting to talk to her. Naturally, her first thought concerns Frederick. She faces the inspector proudly, and he is quite impressed by her. He has come to question her regarding the incident at the railway station which had involved Leonards. In the meantime Leonards has died at the Infirmary, as a result of the fall, and also because his general health was bad as the result of heavy drinking. Before he died he made many unclear remarks about the sea, and about sending a telegraph, and had demanded to see a magistrate. The police have been told that his death had come about when he was pushed by a young man who was accompanied by a lady to whom Leonards had shown some impertinence. This is what one of the porters had seen from a distance. A grocer's assistant had identified the young lady as Miss Hale. Margaret denies that she has been there. She keeps repeating, 'I was not there'. After she opens the door for the inspector to leave, she shuts it, locks it, and then falls in a faint.

COMMENTARY: Because of Margaret's lie, the plot becomes more complicated. Does Frederick's visit serve any other purpose?

NOTES AND GLOSSARY:

Infirmary: a hospital for the poor which was usually run by a religious establishment

inquest: an investigation, here into the death of Leonards

Cornish trick: probably refers to Frederick's ability to knock him down

alibi: an argument that a person charged with a crime was in another place when the crime was committed

Chapter 35: Expiation

Mr Thornton's visit lasts longer than he had expected. Mr Hale finds his company very consoling. He talks to him about his deepest feelings and thoughts, and finds him understanding and helpful, and more deeply religious than he had thought.

In the meantime Margaret is still lying on the study floor in a faint. When she recovers she can only remember two things, that her brother is in danger, and that she has lied to save him. The police inspector had told her that he was coming back, and Margaret decides that if she has heard in the meantime that Frederick is safe, she will tell the inspector the truth.

On leaving the Haleses' house, Thornton meets the police inspector who is coming back. They know each other, and Mr Thornton had been the magistrate called to take down Leonards' confused words. The inspector, seeing Thornton come out of the Haleses' house, tells him the suspicions regarding Margaret, and her denial that she had been at the station at that time. Mr Thornton asks him not to go back to Miss Hale yet, but to meet him at the warehouse in an hour.

Mr Thornton goes to his own private room in the warehouse, and asks that no one be admitted to him. He then gives way to the thoughts that torture him. He tells himself that Margaret must have some shameful action to hide since she denies having been at the station during that incident, when he himself saw her with the young man. Of course he thinks the young man must be Margaret's lover. After a while he decides that no matter how Margaret has behaved, he will save her, and stop the inquest. He leaves a note to this effect for the inspector and goes out.

The inspector is relieved that no inquest is to take place, and he goes to inform Margaret. He also tells her that the decision was based on a note received from Mr Thornton, whom he had informed of the details. Margaret is deeply disturbed at the thought that Mr Thornton now thinks her a liar. Her further thoughts reveal that it has not occurred to her yet that Mr Thornton does not know that the young man was her brother.

Next morning she receives a letter from Frederick, who had seen Lennox in London, and she realises that Frederick was safely out of England at the time she told the lie. She then realises that she had told an unnecessary lie, and it seems to her that she was more upset at appearing a liar in front of Thornton, than in front of God. She begins to suspect her feeling for him.

Frederick's letter reassures his father, who does not know of the incident at the railway station. In his letter Frederick also asks them to keep his visit a secret.

COMMENTARY: Most important here is Margaret's final recognition of her love for Thornton, at a time when his opinion of her must have gone down. The author keeps the reader in suspense by making Frederick ask Margaret not to tell anyone of his visit.

NOTES AND GLOSSARY:

'E par che . . . Sospira!': a quotation from the *Vita Nuova* (1290-4) by Dante (1265-1321) which can be translated as follows: 'And from her lips there comes a gentle spirit, full of love, which says to the soul, 'Sigh' '

Holy of Holies:	originally the 'most holy place' in the Jewish tabernacle where only the High Priest was allowed
livid:	here, colourless

Chapter 36: Union Not Always Strength

Next day Mr Hale and Margaret go to visit Higgins. They find him at home, and out of work, although the strike has ended. He does not want to ask his old employer, Hamper, for work, because one of Hamper's conditions for employing men is that they should not contribute to the Union. Higgins is not willing to accept this condition. He has a strong belief that the Union means strength, and that through it the workers will get their rights. He then talks about Boucher who, in Higgins's opinion, had ruined the chances of the strikers by his role in the riot. He too is now out of work. He had begged Hamper for work and had been turned away. Higgins has no sympathy for him, although his wife and children are starving. Margaret tells him he should never have forced Boucher to join the Union. He would have been better off if he hadn't.

At that moment six men come up the road carrying a dead man. It is Boucher: he has drowned himself. The men ask Higgins to go and inform Boucher's wife, but he cannot do it. Mr Hale is also too weak, and so Margaret offers to go.

Margaret goes and breaks the sad news to Mrs Boucher. With the help of a kind neighbour the children are taken care of.

COMMENTARY: The author makes it clear that Boucher's tragedy is not caused only by the Union, but by his own character.

How many examples can you mention in which Margaret's strength of character is needed to help others?

NOTES AND GLOSSARY:

ill-redd-up:	*(dialect)* untidy
mithering:	*(dialect)* bothering
butty:	*(dialect)* bread and butter
whisth:	*(dialect)* hush

Chapter 37: Looking South

Next day the Hales visit Mrs Boucher again. They find out that Higgins has visited her, but has now gone. Mrs Boucher is a self-centred woman, who sees this tragedy as it affects only herself, and who accuses everybody, including her miserable husband, of conspiring to hurt her. On the way home they talk about her sad situation, and whether town life or country life is harder on people. Then Frederick's visit is mentioned, and Margaret's thoughts turn again to Mr Thornton, and how he must despise her for the lie she has told. She remembers how she had implied in earlier conversations that people in commerce are dishonest.

That evening Higgins comes to see them. He has been looking for work unsuccessfully all day. He feels responsible for Boucher's death, and therefore feels he must take care of his children. It is for them that he needs the money. But no one will give him work. Now he has come to Mr Hale to ask his help in finding work 'in the South'. He has heard Margaret talk enthusiastically about Helstone, and he wants to go and work there. But Margaret convinces him that life is hard when one is working out in the fields, and not as cheap as he thinks.

Higgins realises that North and South, and people everywhere, have problems. Margaret then suggests that he go and ask Mr Thornton for work, and talk to him in person. She is sure Thornton will employ him. And she thinks again what a pity it is that she has lost his respect, just when she has begun to value him.

COMMENTARY: This chapter emphasises again the contrast between North and South. Now the contrast is in favour of the North. This is another sign of the change in Margaret. There is also the more general contrast between town and country.

Sum up what Margaret says in this chapter about life in the South.

NOTES AND GLOSSARY:

redding up:	(*dialect*) tidying up
chivalric:	having the qualities of the ideal knight, relating to chivalry: bravery, honesty, nobility of character
feckless:	weak
fare:	here, food
rucks o'money:	heaps of money
fettle:	(*dialect*) put in order

Chapter 38: Promises Fulfilled

Mr Thornton cannot forget the incident at the station involving Margaret, and he becomes more and more convinced that she loves that man very much if she was willing to tell such a serious lie for him. As we have noticed, Margaret does not know his thoughts about the young man. She is only aware that she has told a lie, and that he knows about it.

In the meantime Mrs Thornton has heard the whole story from her cook who had been engaged to Leonards, and who is convinced that Margaret is involved. Mrs Thornton decides to speak to Margaret, as she had promised Mrs Hale that she would point out to her any wrong-doing, and give her guidance. She too is convinced that Margaret was involved with a young man, and that she wanted to keep this relationship secret.

Margaret welcomes her, and is grateful for what she thinks is to be a friendly visit. Again Mrs Thornton misunderstands Margaret's sweet manner, and when she gets up to leave, she tells her why she has come; namely, to point out to her the impropriety of walking with a young man so far away from home, after dark. She emphasises that many girls have lost their reputation for nothing more than that. And then she mentions her son's proposal, and says that Margaret had rejected him probably because of this other lover. Margaret is insulted and walks out of the room, leaving Mrs Thornton to let herself out.

In the meantime, Mr Thornton is considering how much his business has been hurt by the strike. When Higgins finally gets a chance to speak to him, he is not in the best spirits. The conversation between them is unsatisfactory. Thornton knows about Higgins's role in the strike. Higgins, of course, has come to ask for work, and is at first quite modest. But gradually both get angry and speak to each other very frankly, and finally Thornton turns away without offering him work. Higgins has not mentioned that Margaret has sent him. Thornton's heart is softened, however, when he finds out from the porter that Higgins has been waiting for five hours to speak to him.

COMMENTARY: We can note two points:
(1) The meeting between Mrs Thornton and Margaret, which makes the situation worse. In this connection, notice the irony in the chapter heading.
(2) The meeting between Thornton and Higgins, which, although it also ends in disagreement, has established a contact between these two men, which will eventually lead to a fruitful relationship.

NOTES AND GLOSSARY:
gallivanting: walking about

sharp Damascus blade: sword blade made of hard steel, with special ornamentation, originally from Damascus. The phrase is used here in a figurative sense. The sharp words prepared by Mrs Thornton seem out of place compared with the sweet words of Margaret

beau: an admirer

small beer: something of small importance

Paddy: slang for 'Irishman'

navvy: an unskilled worker

Chapter 39: Making Friends

After Mrs Thornton leaves, Margaret is very agitated. It occurs to her for the first time that Thornton must have taken Frederick for her lover. She finally admits to herself — too late — that she loves him.

Later in the day she goes to visit Mrs Boucher, who is very ill, and then goes to find out from Higgins whether his appeal to Thornton had been successful. While he is telling her of his failure, Thornton arrives to offer him work. He has spent the intervening time finding out more about Higgins, and he is convinced now that he has told him the truth, and that he would be a good worker. They have some more frank words together, and Higgins gladly accepts the work.

As soon as Thornton arrives, Margaret leaves the room, and returns to Mrs Boucher. When Thornton leaves, he meets her. He tells her that he has given Higgins work. He then hints at the incident they are both thinking of, but she does not respond, and they part, both feeling unhappy.

A letter arrives from Mr Bell, announcing his visit to Milton, and one from Edith, announcing that they would soon be returning to London, and are hoping for her visit there.

COMMENTARY: As Mr Thornton gets closer to Higgins, he moves farther away from Margaret. Notice also how the 'point of view' shifts from Margaret to Thornton and back.

NOTES AND GLOSSARY:

'Captain Lennox might sell out': he might sell his commission in the army and return to civilian life. It was customary for a wealthy man to pay to become an officer

upon the tapis: (*French*) under consideration; in the conversation 'tapis' means table cover, carpet

Chapter 40: Out of Tune

Mr Bell's visit proves to be very cheering to Margaret and her father, and he and Margaret get along very well. In their conversations Margaret defends the progressive spirit of Milton against Mr Bell, while he defends the peace and quiet of Oxford. Mr Thornton comes to discuss business matters with Mr Bell, who owns the property in which Mr Thornton has his factory. Thornton's feelings about Margaret give him a great deal of pain; he loves her, but at times tells himself that he hates her. This evening a letter has arrived from Mr Lennox which Mr Hale mentions. Naturally Thornton thinks this is the young man he has seen with Margaret at the station.

The conversation goes back to the ones the Hales and Mr Bell have had about the respective merits of Milton and Oxford. Thornton, of course, defends Milton, and the hard work and enterprise of its people, and denies that their only object is to make money. Something in the conversation then gives Thornton the chance to make a remark which hurts Margaret's feelings. He regrets it right away, and he realises again how much he loves her.

After he leaves, and Margaret goes to bed, Mr Bell suggests to Mr Hale that Thornton and Margaret might be in love. Hale denies this strongly, and Mr Bell thinks he might be mistaken. When he leaves, he invites them both to come and live in Oxford, and assures Margaret that whatever happens, she can count on his friendship.

So Margaret and her father are alone again. Sometimes they visit Higgins, who has taken the Boucher children into his home, after their mother also dies. They talk about Thornton, and Higgins tells them that he cannot understand how a man can have two such different sides to him. On the one hand, he is the strict master. Then he is a human person concerned about other human beings. He often looks in to ask about the Boucher children. On this visit Margaret finds out that he is coming that evening to visit Higgins. So she rushes to leave. But then she regrets it, because she knows her father would have liked to see him. His visits to their house and his lessons with Mr Hale have become so rare that Mr Hale is concerned. Finally he asks Margaret if Thornton had ever expressed his feelings to her, and she admits that he had made her a proposal once which she had turned down. She then turns the conversation to lighter matters, and mentions that her aunt and cousin and her husband and the new baby would be back in London the next day. Mr Hale suggests that she should go and visit them; the change would do her good. She could also see Mr Lennox and find out more about Frederick's case. Margaret will not think of leaving her father, and she is also giving up hope that Frederick would ever be able to clear his name.

As she thinks of her father later on, she decides that he is the one who needs the change. His spirits and health have both been affected by her mother's death, and there was little left to interest and challenge his mind.

COMMENTARY: We are shown another contrast: Milton and Oxford. We are introduced to a new character: Mr Bell. He has been mentioned before, but now he actually appears on the scene, and participates in the story. There is also a growth of understanding between Thornton and Higgins.

NOTES AND GLOSSARY:

Heptarchy: a confederacy of seven Anglo-Saxon kingdoms supposedly established in the seventh and eighth centuries

worshippers of Thor: Thor was one of the gods of the Norse people. Mr Bell here means that the people of Milton are backward-looking, looking to the past

Pearl: in Greek, Margaret means pearl

craddy: (*dialect*) difficult thing

Kilkenny cat's tail: an allusion to a cruel sport practised in Kilkenny, Ireland, around 1800 by Hessian soldiers, in which the tails of two cats were tied together, and the cats made to fight till they died. The sport was forbidden, but was practised illegally. On one occasion, to evade being caught, the soldier cut through the knot to separate the two cats. He then explained to the officer that the two pieces of tails were all that was left after the cats had eaten each other

'the Una from the Duessa': two women characters in the *Faerie Queen* (1589-96) by Edmund Spenser (1552?-99). Una was beautiful and good and represented true religion. Duessa, who was also beautiful but evil and two-faced, represented falsehood

a home question: a vital, central question

Chapter 41: The Journey's End

Mr Thornton's visits have become rarer, though his only reason seems to be his business affairs, which have become more complicated since the strike. It becomes clear that Frederick's case will never be settled, and he gives up England as his native country, especially after his marriage to Dolores Barbour, whose father is a successful business-man. Upon his marriage, Frederick joins the business as a junior partner. Margaret remembers how she had looked down on business before.

An invitation comes for them to visit Mr Bell in Oxford. Margaret insists on letting her father go by himself, as she needs the rest and change of being by herself at home. This gives her the opportunity to think of her own life again, and she remembers the lie she told, and how unnecessary and harmful it turned out to be. She then finds out from Martha, the servant whom Mrs Thornton had recommended, that Fanny is getting married. Martha also says something to her about the kindness and helpfulness of Mrs Thornton when she and her sister were left all alone.

That evening she visits the Higgins family and finds out that Mr Thornton is away on a trip. When she returns home she sorts out some of Henry Lennox's letters, and finds herself thinking of her father with anxiety.

That same evening, in Oxford, Mr Hale is also thinking of his daughter, and wondering what will happen to her if he should die. Mr Bell tells him not to think of death, but promises to take care of Margaret, as he has decided to make her his heir anyway. That same night Mr Hale dies in his sleep. Mr Bell, shocked by this tragic event, decides to go in person to Milton to tell Margaret.

On the train he meets Thornton, who is returning from a business trip to France. He tells him the sad news, and Thornton wonders what will now become of Margaret. Bell tells him that he would like to have her come and live with him, but that she has relatives. He then mentions Lennox to him, and says that he was interested in marrying Margaret, but that he was only kept back by her 'want of fortune'. Now he, Bell, intends to leave her his money, so that would remove the obstacle.

Margaret is standing at an upstairs window, when she sees Mr Bell arrive alone. She knows immediately that her father has died.

COMMENTARY: The death of Mr Hale isolates Margaret almost completely. Besides this we can notice:
(1) Frederick becoming a 'tradesman'; ·
(2) reference to Mrs Thornton's kindness by Martha, the maid;
(3) Margaret choosing the 'way of humility' (in contrast to the 'pride' which we have learnt to associate with her);
(4) Bell's mention of Henry Lennox as a possible suitor of Margaret. The first three points mentioned above serve to bring Margaret closer to Thornton, but the last presents a new obstacle.

NOTES AND GLOSSARY:
unnative himself: make himself the native of another country
preux chevalier: (*French*) gallant knight
'Je ne voudrais . . . aydera.': (*French*)The contents of this passage might be summed up as follows: 'I do not want to scold my heart for its treachery to God. I would rather throw myself on the mercy of God, and start again on the way of humility'
pis aller: (*French*)a last resort
scouted: here, made fun of
to blubber: to weep noisily

Chapter 42: Alone! Alone!

Mr Bell writes to Mrs Shaw telling her the sad news, and urging her to come and take care of Margaret, who is quite stunned by the blow. Mrs Shaw comes with the intention of taking Margaret back to London with her right away, but Margaret insists that she has to have time to say good-bye to her Milton friends.

When Mr Thornton comes to enquire about her, he finds that there is no room for Mr Bell, and invites him to stay with them. Mrs Thornton gives him a warm welcome. In the course of the conversation he mentions Frederick. This is the first time that Thornton has heard of him. Bell tells him all about Frederick. He does not know that Frederick has been in England at his mother's death. So when Thornton tries to identify the young man he saw with Margaret as her brother, Bell assures him that Frederick had not been in England all this time.

The talk turns from Margaret to business, and Thornton tells Bell of the steps he has taken to improve the condition of his workers. He is providing them with a dining room where they can buy meals more cheaply; and on the whole he is getting on much better with them. He owes much to Higgins in this improvement of his relations with the men.

COMMENTARY: Thornton is beginning to see his workers in a more human way. His and Margaret's views are coming closer. But she is about to leave his life.

NOTES AND GLOSSARY:

vis inertiae:	(*Latin*) sluggish; her laziness, her unwillingness to move
savoir faire:	(*French*) tact, social talent
cavalierly:	here, dismissing an important matter in a casual, offhand way
driven to bay:	driven to a position from which it is not possible to retreat; here, forced to answer
mocking bird:	a bird, of the thrush family, which can imitate the sounds of other birds
white wand:	here, a stick used by magicians. Mr Bell probably means that by tasting the food, Thornton could make it taste good
stumbling blocks:	obstacles

Chapter 43: Margaret's Flittin'

Mr Bell writes from Oxford, where the funeral of Mr Hale is taking place, reassuring Margaret that he will always be her friend, and arranging to give her enough money to live comfortably.

Margaret decides to make two good-bye visits before she leaves Milton. Her aunt insists on accompanying her. She first visits the Higgins family. Then they call on Mrs Thornton. Margaret apologises to Mrs Thornton for the way she had spoken to her at their last meeting, and assures her that, although she still cannot explain her conduct, she is not guilty of anything wrong.

Just as they are about to leave, Thornton comes in. Knowing that Margaret is about to leave Milton, he is tempted once more to declare his love. But he hardens his heart and says goodbye.

COMMENTARY: Now things move very fast. Margaret leaves Milton.
If Mrs Gaskell's intention had been to write an 'industrial novel', or

a 'social novel' only, the book could have ended here. But she was also interested in the human element, the 'love story'; so she has to find a way of bringing Thornton and Margaret together again.

NOTES AND GLOSSARY:

Flittin':   flitting, moving from one place to another
confectionery: sweets
Adam Bell: an outlaw mentioned in a ballad in Percy's *Reliques of Ancient English Poetry* (1765). This was a collection of old ballads, songs and romances

---

Chapter 44: Ease not Peace

Margaret returns to London, and to her aunt's luxurious house in Harley Street. Everyone is kind to her. Mrs Shaw wants to get her new clothes; Edith wants to make her feel more comfortable; Captain Lennox is very kind. He spends hours talking to his wife and playing with his son, and the rest of his time at his club, or dining out. Margaret cannot help seeing the contrast between the leisurely and lazy life in Harley Street and life in Milton. Even the servants are out of sight, so that one is hardly aware of anyone working. Margaret does not feel at home any more, and her mind often goes back to Milton. She hears from Dixon, who has stayed behind to sell the furniture and finish all the affairs, and she often wonders if anyone is thinking of her. One evening, while she is alone in the house, Mr Bell is announced. He mentions having come up on the train with Henry Lennox, and he is interested in Margaret's reaction to this news. Mr Bell has just come from Milton, and he tells her how helpful Thornton has been in settling her affairs there. Later in the evening Henry Lennox comes to call. Margaret thanks him for his efforts on behalf of Frederick, and then refers to Frederick's visit to England. Bell is surprised to hear this, and then remembers that someone had asked him this very thing recently, but he does not mention Thornton's name.

Captain Lennox, Edith, and Mrs Shaw return before Mr Bell and Henry Lennox leave. It is agreed that both men are to come for breakfast next morning, because Mr Lennox wants to show Bell and Margaret some papers relating to Frederick's case.

Mr Bell and Lennox walk part of the way together. Mr Bell mentions Margaret, and the talk turns to her father. It becomes clear to Mr Bell that Lennox cannot understand what had prompted Hale to give up the living he had in Helstone. He is too worldly to understand how a matter of conscience can force a man to make such a serious decision.

COMMENTARY: This chapter is in some ways a 'return to the beginning'. Nothing has changed here; even Henry Lennox reappears. But Margaret has changed, and she sees everything with new eyes. Contrasts are emphasised again, as seen through her consciousness, between London and Milton, the places, the people, and the lives they lead. And, implicitly, Captain Lennox and Thornton are contrasted. A more significant contrast, not yet developed, will be between Henry Lennox and Thornton. The last few paragraphs in this chapter reveal something about the character of Lennox.

NOTES AND GLOSSARY:

on circuit:	a journey through certain appointed areas where courts are held
Vashti:	a queen in the Old Testament (Esther, I) who defied her husband, King Ahasuerus
eloquence du billet:	skill in writing notes, or short letters
threw the ball back:	here, answered in the same way
Mordecai:	a man in the Old Testament who adopted Esther, an orphan girl, who later married King Ahasuerus, after Vashti (Esther, II). Edith sees the relationship between Bell and Margaret in the same way as the one between Mordecai and Esther
Quixotism:	idealism or chivalry, carried to an impractical limit (after the hero of *Don Quixote* (1605) by Cervantes (1547-1616))

Chapter 45: Not All a Dream

The conversation with Henry Lennox makes Mr Bell think of Helstone. That night he dreams of Helstone, and of the visit he paid there to his newly married friend Hale twenty-five years ago. In the dream they are both young and happy. He wakes up to feel as if the present is a dream. He hurries on to Harley Street. Lennox gives him and Margaret details about Frederick's case, and tells them of the impossibility of getting the right witnesses to give him a fair trial. Finally Margaret can listen no more. Lennox consoles her by saying that Frederick is now well and happy.

Before he leaves, Mr Bell tells Margaret that he intends to go to Helstone on the following day, to look at the old place again. He invites Margaret to go with him.

COMMENTARY: This is the shortest chapter in the novel. The story seems to take a circular turn here: London-Helstone-Milton-London — and now Helstone again. In the next chapter the author's intention will become clearer.

NOTES AND GLOSSARY:
lachrymal ducts: tear ducts

Chapter 46: Once and Now

Next day Margaret and Mr Bell go on their planned visit to Helstone. As they pass through the railway stations, Margaret notices how much less life there is here than on the busy railway lines between London and the North. The closer they come to Helstone, the more strongly Margaret remembers the past. They drive to the Lennard Arms, an inn in Helstone, where they intend to spend the night. The landlady recognises Margaret, and greets her warmly. She is sad to hear of Mr Hale's death. She had heard about Mrs Hale's death from a gentleman who had been in Helstone in the spring. She is also eager to discuss the new vicar, Mr Hale's successor, and the many changes he has introduced, of which she does not seem to approve.

Margaret sees many changes as she goes for a walk through the village. Many landmarks have disappeared; and the old man whom she had sketched the day Lennox had visited them is dead. She calls on old acquaintances and is horrified when she hears a story about an old woman, Betty Barnes, who had burnt a cat, thinking that would work magic. Margaret sees that some horrible superstitions are mixed in with the simplicity and kindness of the village people. She goes to visit the school, where she finds the vicar's wife in charge. This lady invites her to the vicarage to see the alterations they have made. Margaret now sees that her old home is also not the same any more.

All in all, her visit to Helstone and her old home is not what she had expected. There are many changes. But of course, she has changed too.

That evening as she and Mr Bell are sitting alone, Margaret tells him what has been on her mind for so long. She relates to him the whole incident at the railway station, and that she told Mr Thornton a lie. She wants Mr Bell, if he should ever have a chance, to explain her reasons to Thornton. She does not expect to see Thornton again, but she does not want him to continue to think of her as a liar. Mr Bell assures her that what she did was not wrong, and he promises to explain to Mr Thornton. Next day, Margaret is eager to return to London. Before they leave, she goes back to the vicarage garden and gathers some honeysuckle.

After a few days, when she has regained her calm, she decides that, although she will always love Helstone, she will never go and visit it again.

COMMENTARY: Margaret returns to her beloved Helstone with great longing. But she is disappointed. As the chapter-title indicates, something important has changed. Margaret sees the village and its people with new eyes, and she realises their imperfections. The author intends this visit to be a further step in Margaret's growth and maturing. She can now put the past behind her.

Explain in one or two paragraphs why Margaret decides not to go back to Helstone.

NOTES AND GLOSSARY:

Idyl: here, a literary work that deals with rural life and suggests peace and contentment

Herman and Dorothea: a long poem by the German poet Goethe (1749-1832)

Evangeline: a long poem by the American poet Longfellow (1807–82)

fly: here, a carriage

teetotaller: someone who never drinks alcoholic drinks

'fat and scant o'breath': this is how the Queen describes Hamlet in the fencing scene in *Hamlet*, Act V Scene 2. (There are more allusions to Hamlet in the following lines)

thridded their way: made their way through a difficult path

bosky dell: (poetic language) a small valley full of trees

'wandering sheep of her husband's flock': this refers to the people of the parish, who might be doing something which the pastor does not approve of

'Honi soit qui mal y pense': (*French*) 'Evil to him who thinks evil', the motto of the Order of the Garter, the highest English order of knighthood

jack-in-a-box: a box out of which a figure jumps when it is opened

'as the fisherman coaxed the genie': in one of the Arabian Nights stories a fisherman persuades a genie, a supernatural spirit with magic powers, to go back into the bottle from which he had freed it

---

Chapter 47: Something Wanting

Dixon finally comes to take up her post as Margaret's maid. She brings news of Milton. At last Margaret has someone to talk to about Milton, although Dixon does not like the subject very much.

Margaret is longing to hear from Mr Bell, to know whether he has gone to Milton, and whether he has given the explanation to Thornton. But Mr Bell has not yet decided to make this visit, and his letters show a certain dissatisfaction with life. At one point Edith mentions to Margaret that Mr Bell had once spoken of taking her to visit her brother in Spain. Margaret would very much like to do that, but as Mr Bell had never mentioned any such idea to her, she cannot ask him about it.

In the meantime life for Margaret in the Lennox household is becoming dull and meaningless. There seems no purpose to the life of Edith and her husband, and Margaret thinks that Henry Lennox, who often visits them, shares her views. He himself is hardworking and ambitious, and constantly looking for opportunities and connections that will help him fulfil his ambitions.

He and Margaret meet often, but do not talk much. Margaret feels that, although they have drifted apart, he is still eager to hear her opinions, and to win her approval.

NOTES AND GLOSSARY:

aristocratic bias: favouring the aristocracy

spleen: an organ near the stomach, which was thought to be the source of the emotions; here, melancholy, or bad temper

Chateau en Espagne: (*French*) 'Castle in Spain'; a daydream, something one dreams of but cannot attain

'his good blue-sashed moods': when he was dressed up, and on his behaviour. A blue sash, or belt, was often part of the clothing of a well-dressed child of a well-to-do family

Chapter 48: 'Ne'er to be Found Again'

Edith continues to give dinner-parties to which many clever men are invited. But Margaret begins to feel that all their cleverness and wit are wasted in a frivolous manner, and that they seldom touch on subjects that really matter. Her impatience is increased by the fact that Mr Bell has apparently not gone to Milton. Finally she receives a letter telling her that he was coming up to London to see a doctor, and her suspicions are confirmed that his health is bad. He does not arrive on the day appointed. Next morning Margaret receives a letter from his servant telling her that Mr Bell was very sick and not expected to live.

Margaret insists on leaving for Oxford immediately, but Edith and her mother delay her, so that she misses the first train. When she does finally go, accompanied by Edith's husband, she hears that Mr Bell has died during the night.

All the way back home Margaret thinks of the heavy losses she has suffered this past year. She is grateful for the love and attention with which Edith welcomes her back.

That night, when all the serious thoughts return to her, she realises that it is not enough to will to be good and heroic, but that prayer is also necessary. And she prays that God will give her the strength to always speak and act the truth.

COMMENTARY: This chapter and the previous one reveal more about Henry Lennox's character and his ambitions. But another death occurs, that of Mr Bell. This opens the way to Margaret's wealth. She also now stands quite alone, but she has developed the maturity and inner strength to do so.

Chapter 49: Breathing Tranquillity

One week after Mr Bell's death, Margaret is informed by the lawyer that she is his principal heir, and that the money and property he left are far more than she had expected. It is only natural that Henry Lennox should become her legal adviser, and Edith hopes that they will eventually marry. Lennox hopes so too, but he proceeds very carefully, because he does not want to fail a second time.

Margaret accompanies Mrs Shaw and the Lennoxes to the seaside resort of Cromer, for a change and rest. While there, she has time to think of her life; and although she has now lost all hope that Thornton will ever hear the truth about her, she relaxes enough to see her past life in the right perspective, and to plan the future. She decides, for one thing, to be more independent in future, and to plan her life as she wants.

Of course her money makes her attractive to many men, but her relatives try to keep them all away, except Henry.

COMMENTARY: This is a continuation of the last chapter. Margaret has now become mature and independent.

NOTES AND GLOSSARY:

residuary legatee: the one who will inherit everything after all debts and other legacies have been paid

legacy: something received from an ancestor, or from the past, or in a will

farouche: wild, very shy

Zenobia: ambitious queen of Palmyra, who lived in the third century AD, and captured much of Asia Minor and Egypt before she was defeated by the Romans

Cleopatra: queen of Egypt, in the first century BC, who conquered the Roman victors by her charm and cleverness

conclave: assembly, meeting

Chapter 50: Changes at Milton

Meanwhile in Milton, the factories continue to work and produce goods. But there is worry in the town, because there is news of bankruptcies in other places, and there is news of bad speculations in the United States. So far in Milton no one has failed (become bankrupt), but Thornton feels the danger to his business. The strike had affected his business badly, and much of his capital has been spent on new machinery. It is very difficult for him to accept this danger to his secure position, and to the name and reputation of honesty he has established over the years. There is another important matter that is threatened, and that is his newly found understanding with the workers. Thanks to Higgins, he has managed to build up a strong relationship with the workers, which he will have to give up if the business fails.

One day Higgins asks him if he knows anything about Miss Hale, and he finds out that the young man he saw that day with Margaret was indeed her brother. The property which Margaret had inherited from Mr Bell included the property in which Thornton's factory is located, and so he has become her tenant, and there is a business, if not a personal, contact between them.

Thornton's business troubles only increase and he finally decides, in order to be honest toward his workers and his creditors, to give up his business rather than declare himself bankrupt and so ruin them. This will keep his name clear and respected. His mother agrees with him, although it is a great blow to her. He decides to find employment in somebody else's business.

COMMENTARY: While Margaret becomes rich, Thornton becomes poor. There is a balancing movement here, but also a certain irony. (Remember that Mrs Thornton warned her son not to fall in love with a penniless girl.)

It is Higgins, whom Margaret was responsible for introducing to Thornton, who reveals to Thornton the secret surrounding Frederick. Thornton can now think of Margaret with complete love again, but with no hope of ever marrying her.

NOTES AND GLOSSARY:
failed: here, gone bankrupt
failure: here, bankruptcy
the fine point of the wedge: a small beginning which may lead to something greater
potter: (*dialect*) bother, worry
nobbut: (*dialect*) nothing but, only

Chapter 51: Meeting Again

Not long after, Thornton goes to London to discuss the question of subletting the property with Lennox, who acts as Margaret's business adviser. Lennox invites him to dinner at his brother's house, partly because he wants to be polite to him, and partly because Mr Colthurst, a Member of Parliament, who is very much interested in Milton, is going to be present.

Thornton is still the same distinguished looking man Margaret remembered. But she finds him looking older and careworn. They meet like old friends, and he immediately thinks that there is a relationship between Lennox and her.

The dinner is a success. Thornton impresses Mr Colthurst with his knowledge, his attitude towards his workers, and his experiments with improving his relations with them. Thornton also tells him frankly that he has been unsuccessful in business, and that unfortunately he is going to have to give up his factory and find employment. He hopes it will be possible for him to continue to use the experience he has gained. He believes that there should be much more personal contact with the workers, and that they should be drawn more into the plans of the masters.

As Mr Lennox is leaving, Margaret asks him if she may see him the next day on some important business. His hopes are growing that she might soon agree to marry him.

COMMENTARY: Margaret and Thornton meet again for the first time in a year. They have both changed; they have come closer in their views. Margaret sees Thornton in the company of 'gentlemen', and she realises that he is superior to them.

In your own words, describe how Thornton now appears to Margaret.

NOTES AND GLOSSARY:

'cash nexus': economic or money link; a phrase made popular by Thomas Carlyle (1795-1881) in the nineteenth century, which describes the impersonal relationship between employer and employed. Thornton is emphasising the importance of the personal relationship

round-robin: a petition, a letter asking for something, signed by many people

---

Chapter 52: 'Pack Clouds Away'

Next morning Henry has a long talk with Margaret. When he leaves, Edith realises that nothing personal has been settled. She is disappointed because she wanted Margaret to marry him and stay close by her. Lennox tells her he is coming back next day with Mr Thornton to discuss some plans with Margaret.

Next morning Lennox does not show up. Thornton is received by Margaret. She tries to explain to him the plan she has worked out with Lennox. She wants to lend him the money, at a better interest rate than she is receiving at the bank, so that he can continue to run his business. When she stops talking, Thornton is overcome again by his love for her. Her understands from her silence that this time he will not be rejected, and that now his love is returned. And so the novel moves towards a happy ending.

COMMENTARY:

(1) The novel ends where it begins. It begins with a wedding, it ends with an engagement. The similarity only emphasises the change in Margaret.

(2) Mrs Shaw and Mrs Thornton are both mentioned in the last lines. They are the older generation, representing class-consciousness. The young represent social change and the emphasis on character and ability. They also represent the union of northern manufacturing life and the southern agricultural and land-owning classes.

(3) There is also irony in the fact that now he is penniless and she is rich.

Why, in your opinion, does Margaret prefer Thornton to Henry Lennox?

Part 3

Commentary

Nature, purpose, achievement

When Elizabeth Gaskell began to write her novels, the novel as an art form was already firmly established in England. This meant that she found a ready reading-audience for her novels, made up of readers who knew what to expect of her books because they knew what a novel was. A novel is a piece of prose fiction, dealing with daily life, and, unlike the romance so popular in the Middle Ages, imitating as closely as possible the psychology, events, and setting of real life. Its characters and their problems were expected to be realistic; and there was no room for supernatural or magic elements in the solution of the conflicts, problems and mysteries. Unlike the heroes of the older types of fiction before the novel, the hero, or heroine, of the novel was an individual, not a representative of mankind, or the personification of a virtue or a vice. He or she had a real name, a past, a future, and a specific place and time (the setting) in which he or she lived.

The great changes of the nineteenth century, industrial growth, political reform, and growth of urban life, provided the novelist with a great challenge and new material. These changes placed the individual, especially in the cities, in a situation in which he often found himself isolated, faced by problems which he had to solve alone. The novelist, interested in the individual and his unique life, found much ready-made material for his plots.

Elizabeth Gaskell, then, was no innovator. She used the novel as she found it. But she had definite ideas about what constituted a good novel. In a letter to a young man who had sent her his first novel to review, she gave the following advice:

> . . . every day your life brings you into contact with live men and women . . . Think if you can not imagine a complication of events in their life which would form a good plot . . . The plot must grow and culminate in a crisis; not a character must be introduced who does not conduce to this growth and progress of events. . . . If you but think eagerly of your story till *you see it in action*, words, good simple strong words, will come . . .

She dealt, usually, with contemporary materials, and, as we shall see, she contributed a few well-written and well-constructed novels to the great number of good nineteenth century novels. We cannot claim for her, however, as we can for her contemporaries, Charles Dickens (1812–70) and George Eliot (1819–80), that she advanced the novel in structure, style, unforgettable characterisation, or profound thought. But she remains worth reading for her unique qualities.

North and South, Mrs Gaskell's fourth novel (not counting some short stories and a novelette), is a novel which explores the social and economic problems of mid-nineteenth century England. It concentrates on labour relations in the cotton-mill industry in Manchester; and in so doing presents conflicts and reconciliations, not only between workers and masters, but also, as the title suggests, between the industrial, energetic, aggressive North, and the rural, conservative, gentle South. It is a novel which may be classed among the 'novels with a purpose' or 'social novels' of that era, because its purpose was to present the problems and conflicts which were arising between rich and poor as a result of the changes brought about by the Industrial Revolution. She hoped that, if more people knew about these problems, and could see both sides of the question, something would be done to reconcile the two sides. Mrs Gaskell was not a revolutionary. She is not suggesting that the differences between the rich and poor, the upper classes and the lower classes, can be eliminated. She accepted the fact that there will always be the rich and the poor, or at least the rich and the not-so-poor, the employers and the employed; but she believed in justice and fairness for everyone, and that a reconciliation and an understanding between the two sides would benefit them both.

In this novel the master-worker relationship is represented by John Thornton, the manufacturer, and Nicholas Higgins, one of the workers. The other 'conflict', between North and South, is represented by John Thornton and Margaret Hale, a young girl brought up in London and the rural South, who, in spite of her relative poverty, feels socially superior to Thornton.

Mrs Gaskell's achievement in this novel is that she has shown, through sympathetically represented and well developed and individualised characters, how these various conflicts can be reconciled. The novel, as we shall see, is constructed around these conflicts, and many other contrasts and balances of different kinds.

Historical and sociological background

Social change

North and South is a realistic picture of life in England in the mid-nineteenth century. Its setting, its characters with their preoccupations and conflicts, economic, social, and religious, its theme, all reflect the background against which Elizabeth Gaskell lived and wrote.

Although the novel begins and ends in London, the main action takes place in Milton. Milton has always been identified with Manchester. During the century before this novel was written, there had been a great shift of population from the country to the city, and as a result, the South, which had been the advanced and heavily populated part, became poorer and gave way to the North, which now became rich and influential. Many people from the South, like Margaret Hale in this novel, were inclined to look down on the North, and to consider it inferior because of its aggressiveness, its eagerness to make money, and its new wealth. In fact, the conflict between North and South is very well symbolised by Thornton and Margaret: he, hardworking, independent, a self-made man; she, refined, with an old tradition behind her, but now penniless.

Thornton is an exceptional representative of his class. The industrial and middle classes had had quite a struggle to gain political privileges; and to force the government to remove the protective laws (controls on imports and exports) which put obstacles in the way of business. By the 1850s, they had established themselves fairly securely, although of course there were always the ups and downs of markets, prices, and wages. But many of these men had kept the aggressive and ruthless spirit which had made them rich and powerful. They are often depicted in novels, as they undoubtedly were in real life, as the heartless enemies of the poor. Dickens has created many characters of this kind, and so has Mrs Gaskell herself in *Mary Barton*. But Thornton is different. Although he is powerful and tough, he is fair and honest, and willing to change.

The workers were not the only class which viewed the manufacturers with suspicion. The upper middle classes, the land-owning aristocracy with their inherited wealth, saw in them dangerous rivals whom they would like to look down upon, but could not, because they were becoming too powerful. The last two chapters in *North and South* show Thornton among this class of people. They are surprised at his gentlemanliness and intelligence, and they have to admit his worth. Mr Colthurst, the Member of Parliament, listens to his views on labour relations with respect and interest.

Milton presents other aspects of the conflict as well. Besides showing the poverty and lack of security of the poor, as represented by Boucher, for example, it also shows what the trade unions were beginning to do for the workers—for Higgins, for example. It is true that in *North and South* the Union fails in its objective, but Higgins's viewpoint is presented very persuasively, and he does not lose his faith in what the Union stands for. Trade unions had been started in the eighteenth century. They had been banned for a while, then revived. However, when this novel was written (1855) they had not yet won for the workers the right to strike.

Religion

Religious movements were also doing something to help the poor. Methodism, which had started out as a reform movement in the Established Church, the Church of England, and which had then left that church and become one of the Nonconformist churches, made it one of its main duties to help the poor, and had been among the leaders in social and educational reform. It provided educational facilities for the workers, and taught them to organise.

In *North and South* the Nonconformists do not play any major role, unless we count Bessy's 'methodee fancies', as her father calls them. She apparently belongs to a fundamentalist Methodist group where she had been converted. She quotes the Bible constantly and looks forward to death without fear. It is likely that Higgins himself at one time belonged to such a group, to which he owes the fact that he is relatively well educated. The Union had also taught him a great deal, of course.

Mrs Gaskell herself grew up and lived all her life in a liberal religious atmosphere. *North and South* shows how her religious tolerance and charity extended to all groups. Her father had been a minister in the Unitarian church, but had left it on conscientious grounds (as Margaret Hale's father leaves the Established Church). Much of the literature of the day, including autobiographical writing, tells about people leaving the church, or at least feeling temporary doubts. For example, the novelist George Eliot rejected the religious teachings of her childhood; and Tennyson speaks of despair and doubts in *In Memoriam* and other poems. This was in part the result of new philosophical ideas, and of new scientific theories. Darwin's theory of evolution, for instance, had shaken the faith of many people. However, the men and women who left the Church, whether it was the Established Church or a Nonconformist Church, usually continued to think of themselves as Christians; it was not the moral teachings they rejected, but some of the more rigid dogmas which seemed to them to conflict with their new knowledge or their conscience. (Mr Hale remains a good Christian, believing in God, helping his fellowmen.)

Education

Education had expanded and was reaching many more people, thanks to government reforms, religious organisations, and the unions. Among the facilities available to those not fortunate enough to get a good education in their youth, there were many 'mechanics' institutes' at which skilled workers ('mechanics') could continue their technical education in the evening. There were also people like John Thornton, who had left school at an early age in order to go to work, and who now had time enough to continue their studies. He takes lessons with Mr Hale, not in technical matters, but in the Classics. This 'classical education' was considered a luxury, and a sign that one could afford to turn to something not strictly to do with work, to be a 'gentleman'. (It is an ironic touch that neither Margaret nor Mrs Thornton, for different reasons, approves of these lessons; they agree on little else.)

Family life

Mrs Gaskell usually depicts small families, which normally have one or two children, as we see in *North and South*. (These families are, perhaps, not typical, for the usual Victorian family was large.) The role of women, the relationship between the sexes, the social distinctions even among servants, are faithful pictures of real life. The father in the family, on the other hand, is not the domineering Victorian father, known from real life and from fiction. Mr Hale is kind and gentle. Higgins, the working-class man, is also considerate towards his two daughters. Mrs Gaskell must have drawn on her own experience and observation in portraying them.

Mrs Gaskell is one of the first novelists to mention the railways so extensively. The first railway line had been opened in 1825, and by the middle of the century the railway had covered most of the country, bringing with it revolutionary changes in the lives of the people and the economic and political structure of the country.

It is easy to get from a careful reading of *North and South* a clear picture of England in the mid-nineteenth century. For although most of the action is set in the industrial North, we also have the contrast of the rural South, and of London, which was then and is still the centre of political power and fashionable life.

Structure and plot

By structure we mean the design or form of the novel, the way in which the different parts are related together to make up the whole. By plot we mean the sequence of events and their cause and effect relationship. It is difficult at times to separate structure and plot.

It is significant that *North and South* was written as a serial, appearing in weekly instalments in *Household Words*, which was edited by Charles Dickens. It was the first of Mrs Gaskell's novels to be published as a serial, and we have to take into consideration the problem of writing a serial. As Charles Dickens pointed out to her, a serial story is not a completed novel cut up into so many parts, but a novel constructed in such a way that every instalment is a logical self-contained step forward in the narrative, with an ending which creates in the reader interest and curiosity about the next instalment. This is why, when a novel which was originally serialised is published in book form (as we now read *North and South*) there are bound to be some flaws in the structure. Mrs Gaskell did not like this method of writing, and preferred to think of her novel as a book, and its structure is therefore more like that of a novel published in book form.

North and South is constructed on a system of contrasts. The two main contrasts (and conflicts) and their reconciliation: employer and worker, and North and South (or Thornton and Margaret) have already been mentioned. It is these which make up the main theme of the novel. But the minor contrasts are many and varied, and have already been pointed out in Part 2, in the summaries of the chapters. Here are some of them to reconsider:

1. **contrasts in setting:** London — Helstone
   Helstone — Milton
   Milton — London

2. family relationships: mother — son: Mrs Hale and Frederick,
          Mrs Thornton and John Thornton
          Brother — sister: Thornton and Fanny,
          Frederick and Margaret
          husband — wife: Mr and Mrs Hale,
          Mrs Shaw and her late husband
3. religious views: Mr Hale — Higgs
          Margaret — Bessy
4. characters (character contrasts are usually called 'foils'):
          Thornton — Henry Lennox
          Margaret — Edith
          Margaret — Fanny

The novel begins and ends in the same place (see plot summary, p. 63) — a useful device in revealing the change (another kind of contrast) in the main character, Margaret.

As a reading of the plot summaries shows, the plot of this novel is very carefully worked out. There are actually two plots, which are equally important and closely related. These plots are the reconciliation of master and workers, and the love story of Thornton and Margaret. They are not a main plot and sub-plot.

The author handles these two narrative elements in the novel's plot very skillfully, making sure that the connection between them is not broken, and that the solution of one contributes to the solution of the other. A brief analysis of the plot, without a recapitulation of the events, will illustrate this. The first seven chapters bring Margaret from London to Helstone and Milton, and her meeting with Thornton. In the eighth chapter she meets Higgins and his daughter.

In Chapters 8–21 she gets to know Thornton and Higgins better, and learns much about the North and begins to appreciate it.

Chapter 22 contains the climax, involving both plot lines: the mob scene which breaks up the strike and causes Higgins to lose his job (and later to work for Thornton); and Margaret trying to save Thornton from the mob, and in so doing making him realise his love for her.

Chapters 23 and 24: the events of the last chapter lead to his proposal and rejection.

Chapters 25–36: Frederick's visit, the mother's death, and the incident at the railway station, followed by Margaret's lie, which creates a new obstacle between them.

Chapters 37–39: at Margaret's suggestion, Higgins asks Thornton for a job and starts working for him. Beginning of a new and good relationship.

In this central part of the book (Chapters 22–39) we see events arising out of the strike and the mother's death moving Margaret and Thornton farther apart (the love story), and Thornton and Higgins closer together (the master – worker story).

Chapters 40–42: Mr Hale's death. A new obstacle arises: Thornton is given to understand by Mr Bell that Margaret will now marry Lennox. But she is leaving Milton anyway.

Chapters 43–49: Margaret returns to London. She inherits Bell's money, and the property in which Thornton has his factory.

Chapters 50–52: Margaret's fortunes rise, as Thornton's fall. Higgins tells him about Frederick's visit. He knows now there is no other 'lover', and that her lie was in a noble cause.

We may note these points: Margaret introduces Higgins to Thornton. Higgins removes an important obstacle that is between them. Margaret's money will help Thornton to carry out his work, and his good relationship with Higgins and the other workers.

The plot is realistic, with nothing in it to strain the belief. There are of course coincidences, such as the meeting at the railway station. But isn't it coincidences like this that sometimes create problems in real life? One might also object that the 'happy ending' is contrived, artificial. But Mrs Gaskell has carefully prepared us for it by Margaret's admission to herself that she loves Thornton; and by the connection, mentioned very early in the novel, between Bell and Thornton, and Bell and the Hales.

Since this is a 'novel with a purpose' (called by some critics a 'social novel, or an 'industrial novel'), however, Elizabeth Gaskell does not hesitate to include several chapters in which hardly anything happens, but in which the characters talk about labour problems, the rise or drop in prices, the laws against mutiny at sea, and so on, more to enlighten the reader than the other characters. For example, much of Chapters 10 and 15 concentrates on Thornton's conversation with Margaret and her father on master-worker relations. In Chapter 17 we get Nicholas's views.

Narrative method and style

An author must always decide from whose 'point of view' to tell his story. He (or she) has two choices, a first person 'point of view', in which the story is told in the first person by one of the characters in the story; or a third person 'point of view', in which the story is told by an 'omniscient narrator', that is, a narrator who knows everything. This is the more common narrative method. Many writers, in using this method, intrude into the story themselves, by commenting on certain events, drawing the reader's attention to a certain fact, or moralising in a general way. This is called 'authorial comment'. In her earlier novels, Mrs Gaskell did this often. This is sometimes considered a sign of the writer's lack of skill or lack of experience.

By the time Mrs Gaskell wrote this novel, she had learnt through practice how to handle 'point of view', and could tell a story through a third person 'omniscient narrator' without intruding with 'authorial comment', but yet making the reader aware of her opinions. She retains the 'omniscient narrator' but relates the events mainly through the consciousness of Margaret Hale, the central character in the novel. At the same time, by allowing us glimpses into the minds of some of the other characters, and through conversations between the characters, she gives the reader the chance to see various points of view. The reader is thus spared the often interesting problem which arises when an author presents a first-person narrator and leaves it up to the reader to judge and interpret what such a narrator reports. This sometimes adds a touch of irony or ambiguity to a novel. In *North and South* the reader knows everything, and there is never any doubt what the author wants him to believe.

'Style' is a term which, like 'structure', can be defined in various ways. We use it here to mean the writer's use of language. Mrs Gaskell's style is fluent and straightforward. She does not use irony; she is seldom humorous. Her language is even throughout, without any special effects. It is every-day language used to describe every-day events. Of course she uses figures of speech occasionally (similes and metaphors, for example), and like most writers she often uses nature and the weather in a symbolic way. For example, when Margaret returns to Helstone from London, happy to be back home, 'the weather was sultry and broodingly still'. We can expect something unpleasant to happen. When the family first arrive in Milton, and Margaret is homesick for Helstone, we are told, 'The thick yellow November fog had come on, and the view . . . was all shut out . . .' A few paragraphs later, we read, 'all other life seemed shut out from them by as thick a fog of circumstance'. Clearly, here, the fog is not only a natural phenomenon, but also symbolises their isolation.

There are also many literary allusions, referring to the *Arabian Nights*, to fairy tales, to well-known and little-known ballads and poems. We note also that some of her characters, for instance Higgins, speak in a distinctive, 'personal' manner, which is usually easily identifiable.

A special feature of her language, however, is her use of dialect in distinguishing between the Manchester working class and the other characters. Higgins and his daughters speak the dialect of the area, not 'standard English'. Mrs Gaskell's intention was not to make fun of them, or, on the other hand, to make the dialect better known. She uses it to 'fill in' or 'build up' her characters, and to show how closely linked they are to their background. This is why their language is not difficult to understand. The difficult words have to be explained, especially to the reader whose native language is not English. But in general, the meaning is clear from the context; and the grammar and sentence structure follow standard English pretty closely.

For a contrasting effect, Mrs Gaskell is also fond of using French phrases. These are used by and in connection with the Hales and the Shaws, and their fashionable upper-class friends. This makes a rather interesting contrast, not only with the workers, but also with the Thorntons, who only speak standard English, thus perhaps symbolising this new independent and powerful English class of tradesmen.

Character studies

Margaret Hale

Margaret Hale is the central character of the novel. On one level the novel is about her, how she changed and matured from a proud and biased girl into a self-aware and fair-minded young woman who is able to confess her love.

Since most of the action of the novel is related through her consciousness (but not *by* her), the reader has much opportunity to read her mind and know her thoughts. There are also many comments and thoughts from others about her, as well as direct remarks from the author, so that we get a fairly well-rounded picture of her. One of the adjectives applied to her most often is 'proud'. Sometimes it comes

directly from the author: 'The strong pride that was in her . . . '
(Chapter 3); 'the old proud attitude . . . ' (Chapter 24); 'she replied
proudly . . . ' (Chapter 24); 'hasty . . . proud'. (Chapter 49).
Sometimes we get Thornton's view of her: 'impression of haughtiness
. . . ' (Chapter 7); 'proud disagreeable girl . . . ' (Chapter 10); 'set it
down to pride . . . ' (Chapter 15).

Mrs Gaskell's use of 'point of view', however, prevents the reader
from taking a dislike to Margaret, because we have a chance of
finding out that this pride has many facets and causes. One cause, of
course, is the snobbishness towards the tradesman class with which
she was raised; another is that, thrown into this strange new
environment, Margaret needs this pride as a kind of protection. We
are aware of this in her first meeting with Thornton, and in her
successive meetings with his mother, who is proud herself (see below),
and who does not quite hide her disapproval of Margaret. In the
meeting with the police inspector it is her pride which gives her the
strength to stick to her lie. And the two proposals, both so unexpected,
and at the same time so different, are rejected with a pride which
hurts the feelings of the men.

From these examples we might deduce that Margaret's pride was
almost something instinctive, a feeling she called upon to help her
meet new or embarrassing situations. It is interesting that Nicholas
Higgins, the workman, refers to her 'proud bonny face' (Chapter 8);
that is, he sees the pride and the kind-heartedness at the same time.
Only her close relatives (and the reader) are able to see this. It is this
pride also which prevents Margaret from recognising her love for
Thornton. It is also her pride which makes her tell the truth (except
on that one critical occasion) and often be tactless (as when she speaks
with Mrs Thornton), and which also gives her strength. In the final
scene with Thornton her pride gives way to love, and she says, 'I am
not good enough'.

The other striking trait in Margaret is her strength of character.
We see everyone relying on her and asking her help, especially her
father. She has to break the news to her mother that they are going to
leave Helstone. She helps her father find a place to live in. She
protects her father as long as possible from the news that his wife is
fatally sick. She is called upon to tell Mrs Boucher about her
husband's suicide. She has to carry on when her father and brother
are too upset to think of funeral arrangements. The doctor sees this
quality in her very clearly. He describes her to himself as 'a fine girl

. . . a queen . . . game [brave]', when he sees how she reacts to the
news of her mother's fatal illness.

Margaret is also kind-hearted and religious. We see this in the way
she talks to Bessy Higgins. It is these qualities combined with her
strength which enable her to stand up to Nicholas Higgins and take
him home with her when Bessy dies.

The change in Margaret comes about through her growing realisation that she loves Thornton, and from the fact that after the deaths
of her parents and Mr Bell she finds herself alone, and she is forced to
think about herself, her life, and her future. She wants to keep her old
independence of spirit; she does not want to fit into the aimless life of
her aunt and cousin, but she realises that it does not depend on her
only. 'Not only to will, but also to pray, was a necessary condition in
the truly heroic' (Chapter 48). Since Mrs Gaskell's religious views are
liberal and expressed indirectly and never in the form of a sermon, we
can see this rather general statement as showing Margaret's maturing.
She does not become a boring, pious girl who talks about religion all
the time (like Bessy), but a mature young woman who understands
herself and others better. At this point Thornton returns into her life,
and she is ready to accept and return his love.

Before leaving Margaret, it is neccesary to point out how different
from — and superior to — the other two young girls she is; that is,
her cousin Edith, and Fanny Thornton. (This is a good example of the
use of 'foils' in describing character.) On the other hand, in her pride
and strength she resembles, surprisingly, Mrs Thornton; but she is
gentler and softer, able to show affection and warmth, where the other
is strict and 'just' (see below). Needless to say, like most heroines,
Margaret is also beautiful.

John Thornton

John Thornton, or, as the author in typical Victorian fashion refers to
him, Mr Thornton, is a self-made and ambitious young man who, at
first, represents for Margaret the 'tradesman' class which she looks
down upon. When she first sees him, she describes him as 'tall, broad-
shouldered, neither exactly plain, nor yet handsome . . . not quite a
gentleman' (Chapter 7). The key word here is 'gentleman', and it
takes Margaret a while to realise that, although he does not fit into
her original idea of what a 'gentleman' is, he is in every way superior
to the 'gentlemen' that she knows.

The character of Thornton is revealed through what he says and does, and also through what others say about him. The workers, for example, respect him. Higgins calls him a 'bulldog', that is, a stubborn man, but an honest and fair fighter. As he gets to know him better he sees him as more complex: 'He is two chaps. One chap I knowed of old as were measter all o'er. T'other chap hasn't an ounce of measter's flesh about him' (Chapter 40). Margaret is struck by the contrasting elements in his character from the beginning. 'How reconcile those eyes, that voice, with the hard, reasoning, dry merciless way in which he laid down axioms of trade . . .' (Chapter 19). At the end of the book, when she sees him in the company of London society 'gentlemen', she is struck by his 'noble composure . . . inherent dignity and manly strength . . .' By now she knows she loves him.

Thornton's character can easily be explained by the fact that he had had to struggle hard to get to this position of wealth and power. He had denied himself many things, worked hard and honestly, and had succeeded. He felt that everyone who did this would succeed, and so he was not very sympathetic to the complaints of the workers. But, as we see, he is honest and intelligent enough to see that a change is necessary, and he is not too proud to learn from his workers.

He has been brought up by his mother who is a strong woman and who loves him and is proud of him, but who cannot show her feelings; and so he too finds it difficult to express his feelings. But once he falls in love with Margaret, his love does not change, even though he suffers many disappointments. But this is what we expect from a man who is strong, proud, honest, and hard on himself.

It is difficult to say to what extent Thornton is influenced by his love for Margaret. The change in him is not as great as the change in her, and is to a large extent due to the contact with Higgins and his new understanding of the workers.

The other characters

Of the remaining characters in the novel, **Nicholas Higgins** is meant to represent the working class. But he is more than a mere representative of a class. He is a well-rounded character who is interesting in his own right, and who, unlike most of the other characters, also speaks in quite an individualistic way. It is not only that he speaks in his own dialect, but that he uses picturesque and lively images; and sometimes he speaks in brief, apt sentences. In describing Thornton, 'he'll stick to it like a bulldog' (Chapter 17). 'Good works is scarce and bad words is plentiful.' 'I believe what I see, and no more.' He also speaks in analogies.

He is a good worker, and loyal to the Union. He is also proud, stubborn, and sometimes hasty and quick-tempered. But he has a good heart underneath it all. Margaret has noticed it. She says of him, 'He has a good warm heart under his abrupt ways' (Chapter 35). And his sick daughter Bessy says of him, 'he's a rare good man, is father'.

He is a good father who is surprisingly kind to his two daughters. Like all workers he has had a hard life, and, like most of them, has been taken advantage of by the masters. He has, naturally, become bitter and suspicious. In Thornton he finds an employer who, like him, is proud, outspoken, and honest, and who takes special pride in a job well done. It is not surprising that the two get along and learn from each other.

Mr Hale, Margaret's father, is a clergyman who, for reasons of conscience, leaves his church, and so sets all the events of the novel in motion. After this, however, we don't see him making decisive decisions. He is a scholar, a sensitive and good man. Thornton describes him as 'good and gentle and learned' (Chapter 9). Other adjectives that are applied to him, by others and by himself, are 'meek,' 'kind-hearted,' 'a poor coward'.

He seems to feel responsible for his wife's sickness, and in general feels he has disappointed her, especially by his decision to leave Helstone. He is also weak in critical situations, and depends on Margaret to handle them for him. He does not want to believe that his wife is fatally ill. Altogether this kind and scholarly man is not quite fit to handle the difficulties of life. He is much more at home with books.

Mrs Gaskell herself described him in a letter as follows:

> Mr Hale is not a 'sceptic'; he has *doubts,* and can resolve greatly about great things, and is capable of self-sacrifice in theory; but in the details of practice he is weak and vacillating.

But this does not mean that he does not understand the world. He is interested in everything going on in Milton, and is more openminded than Margaret in understanding the factory owners and the workers. He recognises the worth of Thornton long before she does, and gets along with Higgins much better than Margaret expected.

Mrs Thornton, the mother of John Thornton, is a strong woman who has been her son's main support during the difficult years, and is very proud of him. She takes a dislike to Margaret, mainly because her son has fallen in love with her, but also because she considers her too proud. At the same time she is proud herself. Mr Hale says of her that she is 'as haughty and proud in her way, as our little Margaret is in hers'.

But she is a just and fair woman who wants her son to be happy; and she is always truthful, sometimes more than necessary: 'ungraciously truthful,' as the author says. She is not used to showing affection, and feels that 'all the softer virtues verged on weakness'. She forms a good contrast —'or foil — to Mrs Hale.

Mrs Hale, Margaret's mother, is a kind and pretty woman who is, however, very self-centred, and often insensitive to the feelings of her husband and daughter. The author uses words like 'plaintive,' and 'querulous' to describe her. She becomes ill soon after they move to Milton and dies shortly after. It is because of her great desire to see Frederick, who is her favourite child, before she dies, that Margaret gets involved in the lie which complicates her relationship with Thornton.

Fanny Thornton is Thornton's sister, a vain and silly girl who lacks her mother's and brother's strength of character and ability. She marries an older man who is very rich.

Mrs Shaw, Margaret's aunt and the sister of Mrs Hale, is the widow of a general who had left her a lot of money. She is kind and generous to Margaret, but like Mrs Hale tends to be self-centred and complaining.

Edith Shaw is Mrs Shaw's daughter and Margaret's cousin, a pretty, good-hearted, but spoilt girl with not much will of her own. She too loves Margaret, but does not quite understand her.

Frederick Hale, Margaret's brother, had been an officer in the navy. He had become involved in a mutiny by siding with the sailors against a tyrannical captain, and was afraid to return to England. He does return secretly, however, just before his mother dies. He is a handsome and likeable young man. His mother says of him, 'he was born with the gift of winning hearts'. He does not take life as seriously as Margaret does, and we can't help feeling that he was rather spoilt by his mother and Dixon. His role in the novel seems to be to complicate the relationship between Margaret and Thornton.

Mr Bell is a Fellow at Oxford, a scholar, and a rich man. He is a good friend of Mr Hale and tries to help him. His life at Oxford seems to have made him lose contact with some of the realities and problems of the world.

Dixon has been the maid of Mrs Hale since before Mrs Hale's marriage. She is very attached to the family, especially to Mrs Hale and Frederick, but she is something of a snob, and keeps hinting that Mrs Hale should have married a richer man.

Bessy Higgins is the daughter of Nicholas Higgins. She is dying of a lung disease. She is fanatically religious and keeps talking about death and Heaven. She is concerned about her father and sister, but seems already detached from life.

Mary Higgins is Bessy's younger sister. She is a simple, good-hearted, untidy girl, who works for a few days at the Hales' home during Frederick's visit.

Henry Lennox, an ambitious young lawyer, falls in love with Margaret. He is clever and a 'gentleman', but too worldly for Margaret to return his love.

Captain Lennox, Henry's brother and Edith's husband, is a nice young man, easy, kind and gentlemanly; but when he leaves the army he is quite content with leading a lazy and aimless life.

Leonards was a sailor on Frederick's ship. A bad type who had betrayed the men to the Captain, he is now eager to report Frederick and get the reward. But he does not succeed in this, and dies as the result of a fall.

Dr Donaldson is the doctor who attends Mrs Hale when she becomes very sick and dies in Milton. He has been recommended by Mrs Thornton.

George Watson is the police inspector who questions Margaret about the accident at the railway station involving her brother, Leonards and herself.

Boucher is a workman who commits suicide after he loses his job because of the strike.

Mrs Purkis is the landlady of the 'Leonard Arms' inn, in Helstone, who was glad to see Margaret when Margaret and Mr Bell paid a short visit to Helstone.

Hepworth is the vicar who succeeded Mr Hale in the church in Helstone. He has made many changes, and is an intolerant man.

Colthurst is a Member of Parliament who is interesting in hearing about Milton from Thornton.

Part 4

Hints for study

General study hints

In studying a work of fiction it is always helpful to keep the following basic points in mind:

Setting

Where and when does an event occur? For example where does Henry Lennox propose to Margaret? Does it matter where? What is the weather like? Is it important at that particular moment? Usually when the author mentions the weather, it is significant in some way; maybe it is symbolic of the characters' feelings.

Plot

This is the most obvious element in a work of fiction. What happens, and in what sequence, and what are the cause and effect relationships? What kind of conflict, or conflicts, do we encounter? The conflict may be between two characters—for instance, Margaret and Thornton; or within a character, for instance Margaret in conflict with herself about her feelings for Thornton. The conflict can also be between a character and his environment.

Theme

The theme is the central or controlling idea. It usually expresses a generalization about life. One of the themes in *North and South* might be: understanding between classes of people leads to the prosperity of all.

Character

How are the characters presented: only in the words of the author? Or do they reveal themselves in their actions and speech? What is their role in the plot? What is their relationship with the other characters? Do they change in the course of the novel?

Climax

This is the most dramatic moment in the action, or a major turning point. In *North and South* the mob scene outside Thornton's house when Margaret tries to protect him may be seen as the climax.

In addition, follow these hints:
(1) Read the novel carefully, making use of the glossary and commentary provided with the summary of each chapter. Do not rely on the summaries. They are only aids. Nothing replaces the reading of the novel. Use them for review. You will find it useful to make your own brief summaries of each chapter.
(2) When answering questions, stick to the point. Do not write everything you know.
(3) Make your points clearly, developing each one in a paragraph.
(4) Always refer to specific scenes from the novel to illustrate your answer. If you can find a suitable quotation as well, so much the better. Never generalise.

The following specimen questions and answers may be helpful.

Specimen questions and answers

(1) Why do you think the author decided to end the story where it began, in the home of Mrs Shaw in London?

SOME POINTS: circular movement — back to London where nothing has changed
this emphasises change in Margaret: the union between her and Thornton represents the new age, it is forward-looking contrasted with Edith and Captain Lennox — nice people, but no change, belonging to the past.

In ending the novel where it began, Mrs Gaskell gives it a 'circular movement,' that is, the characters and their action move in a circle: London — Helstone — Milton — and back to London, back to the beginning. This is a neat way of ending her story, because a circle is always complete, leaving nothing out.

But although we 'return to the beginning', very much has happened
to Margaret. In the first place, she moved from the luxury of life at
her aunt's house back to her simple but comfortable home in Helstone,
where she felt she really belonged. But before long, she had to leave
Helstone and move with her parents to Milton in the North, to a new
environment which was different from Helstone, and which she hated
at first. Milton was smoky, busy, loud. People were hard-working and
always in a hurry. They judged her by different standards. Here
nothing was taken for granted. You were judged by what you achieved.
Margaret began to see the value and importance of Milton, and to
understand the pride and ambition of its inhabitants, and she began to
change, and to change her standards. But she had to move again, and
this time back to familiar London. And now this comfortable life,
these elegant people with their leisure and entertainments, don't please
her any more. She feels that they are wasting their lives doing
meaningless things, which do not benefit them or other people. She
compares them with the busy constructive Milton people, who are
forward-looking. Above all, she compares the men with Thornton. She
has changed, but her relatives and her friends have not.

This was the easiest and most effective way of showing us the
changes that had occurred in Margaret. It also makes the ending more
convincing. When Margaret agrees to marry Thornton, she has had a
chance to see London life again, and she decides that it is not really
for her any more. Her place is now at the side of Thornton. To make
this change even more convincing, the author adds the trip which
Margaret takes to Helstone with Mr Bell. There too, things have
changed for Margaret, and she knows she will never feel at home
again there. She is now ready to put the past out of her mind.

We notice also that not only does the book end where it began, but
it ends, as it began, with a marriage about to take place. But this
marriage is different from the first one; it is not traditional, but one
that represents social change and the new age, the reconciliation
between 'North' and 'South'.

(2) How important is the role of Frederick Hale in the novel?

Before answering this question we have to give a brief summary of
Frederick's life and actions, and then see how significant his role is.
Frederick Hale is the son of Mr and Mrs Hale, and the brother of the
main character, Margaret. When the story opens, he is already outside

England, afraid to come home, because he has been involved in a mutiny, and a court martial awaits him if he does return.

We find out from what Mrs Hale says that he is attractive, good-hearted, and brave, and that he became involved in the mutiny because he cared about justice, and wanted to defend the sailors. Frederick does not appear in the story in person until after the middle of the novel. He appears in Chapter 30 and leaves in Chapter 32, which means he appears in three chapters out of fifty-two. He comes secretly to visit his dying mother, and leaves soon after she dies. At the railroad station, just before he leaves, two things happen which have serious consequences:

(1) He and Margaret are seen by Mr Thornton, who assumes that Frederick is Margaret's lover;
(2) He is seen by a former sailor who recognises him and wants to hand him over to the police. They have a scuffle, the man falls, and Frederick gets away.

The consequence of these two incidents is that Margaret, to protect Frederick, has to lie about having been at the station. Thornton knows that she has told a lie, and, not knowing that this young man was her brother, concludes that she has something shameful to hide. This creates a further barrier between him and Margaret, and postpones for twenty chapters the happy ending. It also influences Mrs Thornton's feelings about Margaret.

What would have happened if Frederick Hale had not existed, or had not come to England at that particular time? We can say that Thornton might have had the courage to propose again sooner. But perhaps not, because it needed the deaths of her parents and Mr Bell to give Margaret the realisation that she loved Thornton. As far as Thornton is concerned, even though he knows that Margaret has told a lie, he has to admit to himself that he still loves her. When he finds out from Higgins that the young man he has seen her with was her brother, he is relieved and happy, but by then he has given up hope of ever winning her.

After Frederick leaves England and returns to Spain, he is mentioned quite often because news continues to come from him, and because Henry Lennox, the lawyer, tries to help him to clear his name. Lennox thus has the opportunity of seeing Margaret more often, which gives him hope that she will one day return his love. But this does not work out either.

We see then that although Frederick is an interesting character, and his adventures add some excitement to the plot, his role is not really significant. Without him, Thornton and Higgins would have tried to solve the labour problems which threaten both of them, and without him Margaret would have grown to admire and appreciate the North. The only thing to be affected is the relationship between Margaret and Thornton, which is disturbed by Frederick's visit and is affected only temporarily. Thornton goes on loving Margaret in spite of his suspicions, and, at the end, Frederick is not mentioned between them at all.

(3) Discuss three kinds of contrasts which appear in the novel.

CHARACTER: Margaret and Edith
FAMILY RELATIONSHIP: Mrs Hale — Frederick and Mrs Thornton
                — Thornton
SETTING: Milton and Helstone; the two drawing-rooms

North and South is built up on different kinds of contrasts: character, setting, family relationships, and religious convictions. For character contrasts we shall choose here one example for discussion: the two cousins, Margaret and Edith. It is true that Edith only appears at the beginning and the end of the novel, but whenever she appears the author clearly means to contrast her with Margaret, thus making both characters stand out more clearly. Edith is always made to appear kind and likeable, and fond of her cousin. She is also very pretty, 'a soft ball of muslin and ribbon, and silken curls'. Margaret's beauty is described with words like 'tall, finely made figure', 'lofty serenity', 'large soft eyes'. Margaret's beauty, then, denotes maturity and strength of character, Edith's is childlike and sweet. Margaret returns her cousin's love, and never feels any jealousy of Edith's wealth and her easier life. But it becomes clear that Edith, besides being somewhat childlike, is spoilt and self-centred, while Margaret has to think of others and lend her support to her parents. We see her supporting her father in his trouble, and cheering up Bessy and Bessy's father. We usually see Edith having a nice time, with other people waiting on her and with all her wishes fulfilled. But Mrs Gaskell makes them both attractive and pleasant, and above all, they are good friends. This is why the contrast is so effective.

We could also contrast Margaret with Fanny. Fanny is not as attractive or likeable as Edith, and this is why the contrast is not so successful. But the author emphasises her superficiality (she marries an older man for his money), and her weak character (she is always complaining, and has apparently never done anything useful in her life). Her mother has to admit that Margaret is superior to her in many ways.

Another kind of contrast is in family relationships. We have two mother-son relationships which can be compared and contrasted: Mrs Hale and Frederick, Mrs Thornton and Thornton. Frederick has always been his mother's favourite child, and she has probably spoilt him. His involvement in the mutiny was the result of his strong feelings of justice, so we must see him as a good and strong man (not unlike Thornton in this respect). But Mrs Hale is not a strong woman, and when she knows she is going to die, she is so eager to see him that she does not mind having him risk his life. Her love for him is deep and genuine, but also sentimental and slightly selfish. Mrs Thornton, on the other hand, has been her son's strong support during the years when he had to struggle hard. He, too, was her favourite child. Her love for him is deep and genuine, but she does not express it in sentimental or even in loving words. She is a strong woman who hides her feelings. And she is even prepared to suppress her jealousy and dislike of Margaret if Margaret should marry her son.

One further difference is that Mrs Hale and Frederick have been separated for a long time, and although Frederick loves his mother very much, and risks his life to come and see her, he has already established a life for himself outside England to which he is eager to return. Mrs Thornton and her son, on the other hand, have lived and worked together all these years, and the bond between them is of a different kind.

Finally, as a contrast in setting, we shall discuss not the big contrasts like Milton and Helstone, or Milton and London, but the living-rooms of the Hales and the Thorntons. These living rooms are not only settings, but they serve to reveal the characters of their owners as well. Mrs Gaskell lets us see these contrasts through the eyes of the characters. This is how Thornton sees the Haleses' drawing-room: 'Somehow, that room contrasted itself with the one he had lately left' (Chapter 10). The Thorntons' living-room was expensively furnished, with mirrors and gilding, but with a cold look as if it was not lived in; here there were no mirrors, but old, comfortable furniture, flowers, books, and signs that people lived and worked in it. In a later chapter the Thorntons' drawing-room is described when it is all lit up, ready for the party. But it remains cold and impersonal. The two rooms symbolise the contrast between the two families: the Hales, warm, living close together, and not rich enough to afford new and expensive furniture; the Thorntons, on the other hand, rich enough to buy expensive furniture, but unable to show their personal feelings (like the cold drawing-room), unable to relax and enjoy themselves and forget about work, even in their own home.

These are many more examples to illustrate these kinds of contrast, and other kinds of contrast as well — for example: people's religious views, their language, marriage, and of course the main contrast between North and South. But these three examples show Mrs Gaskell's method very clearly.

Some additional questions

(1) Discuss three kinds of conflict which appear in the novel.
(2) Discuss the role of Nicholas Higgins.
(3) What does the novel tell us about mid-nineteenth century England?
(4) Show how Elizabeth Gaskell succeeds in combining the 'love story' with the 'industrial problems' in this novel.

Part 5

Suggestions for further reading

The text

GASKELL, ELIZABETH: *North and South.* Edited by Dorothy Collins, with an Introduction by Martin Dodsworth. Penguin Books, Harmondsworth, 1970.
GASKELL, ELIZABETH: *North and South.* Edited with an Introduction by Angus Easson. Oxford University Press, London, 1973.

Both editions are easily obtainable and based on good texts; they also provide helpful annotations and introductions.

General reading

CECIL, DAVID: *Early Victorian Novelists; Essays in Revaluation.* Penguin Books, Harmondsworth, 1948 (first published 1934). Contains an interesting but somewhat condescending chapter on Mrs Gaskell.
CRAIK, W. A.: *Elizabeth Gaskell and the English Provincial Novel.* Methuen, London, 1975.
POLLARD, ARTHUR: *Mrs Gaskell: Novelist and Biographer.* Harvard University Press, Cambridge, Mass., 1966.
WRIGHT, EDGAR: *Mrs Gaskell: The Basis for Reassessment.* Oxford University Press, London, 1965. An analytical study of Elizabeth Gaskell's novels, providing much background information, a thematic approach and discussion of technique.

Biography

GERIN, WINIFRED: *Elizabeth Gaskell: a Biography.* Clarendon Press, Oxford, 1976.
HOPKINS A. B.: *Mrs Gaskell: Her Life and Work.* John Lehmann, London, 1952. The standard biography, with a good bibliography.

The author of these notes

ANAHID MELIKIAN was born and brought up in Jerusalem, and educated in the United States, at Wagner College, Staten Island, and the University of Wisconsin. She is the author of *Byron and the East* (American University of Beirut, 1977), and co-editor with Suheil B. Bushrui of a new edition of Byron Porter Smith, *Islam in English Literature* (New York, Caravan Books, 1975).

She is Assistant Professor of English at the American University of Beirut.